Understanding Your Child's Temperament

BEVERLY LAHAYE

KINGSWAY PUBLICATIONS
EASTBOURNE

ISBN 0 85476 760 6

Designed and produced by Bookprint Creative Services
P.O. Box 827, BN21 3YJ, England for
KINGSWAY PUBLICATIONS
Lottbridge Drove, Eastbourne, E. Sussex BN23 6NT
Printed in Great Britain.

Reproduced from the original text by arrangement with
Harvest House Publishers, Eugene, Oregon.

Contents

A Note from the Author

This book may seem somewhat familar to you as you browse its pages, but it is different. The publisher approached me in 1995 to see if I would be interested in revising and updating *How to Develop Your Child's Temperament* (Harvest House, 1977) for today's parents. Amazingly, I had already been thinking about the importance of a project like this. I agreed to move ahead on it as soon as I could work it into my schedule of speaking and traveling for Concerned Women for America.

The basic principles of the four temperaments do not change, but how we apply them to the current needs of today's children has changed dramatically. The challenges that parents are confronted with today as they try to raise their children in a society that is not family-friendly have also changed.

Even if you have used the first edition of this book, I believe you will find this second edition more helpful because it addresses some of the temptations our children are facing today that were not a major problem 20 years ago. In this revision the main purpose, reflected in the new title, is to help you *understand* your child's temperament.

Many thanks to Harvest House for their insight into the needs of children today. It is my prayer that God will use this book to help parents better understand their children and to raise children who will bring honor and glory to Jesus Christ.

1

Mirrors of Our Life

As I turned the corner to enter my bedroom I saw her standing in front of the mirror admiring herself from every angle, wearing one of my finest dresses and my high-heeled shoes. Then she pulled on a pair of my white lace gloves and reached for the tube of red lipstick.

At this point my six-year-old daughter looked more like a clown than the sophisticated lady she was pretending to be. As she reached for my precious French perfume, I entered the room and said, "My, you look lovely; and what is your name?" She turned around and in complete surprise replied, "You know me! I'm Lori! I'm trying to be just like you, Mommy."

I caught my breath and at first wanted to laugh, wondering if that is how she thought I looked. Then a lump rose in my throat as I realized that this child was very serious and was trying to be a copy of me. What a responsibility! What love! What adoration! What a priceless privilege and a great responsibility to have a child who admired me so much that she wanted to be just like me! It caused me to search my heart and ask God to help me be the kind of role model that would lead her steps in the right way. I knew it was my responsibility to protect her from following other role models that would be contrary to what God wanted her to be, because children will look for heroes.

Which Example?

Little boys often try to walk with the same stride as their fathers, or crawl under their tricycles with a tool as they try to be just like Dad. Often they even try to part their hair on the same side as Dad's. (As they get older, though, they wouldn't be caught dead trying to mimic their father—it wouldn't be cool!)

We as parents are to set godly examples for our children, not just in how we walk or dress, but in our morals and values. In today's society there is a growing movement to let the public schools be the "surrogate parent" to raise the children and make decisions in personal values, healthcare, and individual rights. In fact, the book titled *It Takes a Village to Raise a Child,* written by Hillary Clinton, suggests that parents need to have government programs to help raise their children today.

But God's plan for nurturing children is very clear: It takes a mother and father, not the government, to train up children according to God's divine will and instruction to prepare them for adulthood.

This critical period of development in a child's life should not be given to a daycare center, either. For several years our society promoted the idea of mothers going back to work just weeks after their babies were born. Daycare centers became the daily babysitters while mothers pursued their careers or worked to maintain their standard of living. But now, years later, many moms are deciding that it just isn't worth it, and they are returning home to care for their children. There is simply no substitute for a mother's care during those first few years of life to ensure a stable emotional beginning for a child.

Our Reflection

Maybe the reflection of my daughter in the mirror that day some years ago provided a warm reminder to me that she was copying me, her mother, rather than a hired daycare worker. And now, several decades later, I'm glad that I could be there as her role model, for now she has her own daughter following in her footsteps.

Parents truly do leave their reflection on several generations of children after them!

2

Shaping Young Desires

God has given parents the responsibility to love, protect, train, and discipline their children. This requires the commitment of both the mother and the father. Proverbs 6:20 says, "My son, keep your father's command, and do not forsake the law of your mother." Raising a child is most effective when it is done with both parents following the scriptural teaching for child development and character training as they work closely together.

Psalm 127:3,4 tells us, "Behold, children are a heritage from the Lord; the fruit of the womb is His reward. Like arrows in the hand of a warrior, so are the children of one's youth." An arrow needs to be properly aimed or directed to reach its target. Also, the arrow requires a bow for its power.

I have talked with and observed people who excel in the skills of the bow and arrow, and I have noticed that the bow must be brought into subjection and bent in order to properly direct the arrow. This visual aid illustrates the need for parents to properly shape the wills of their children to bring them into subjection and to direct them toward the right target.

Desire Toward Evil

A child's nature is twofold: toward evil and toward good. Psalm 51:5 gives the first characteristic: "Behold, I was brought forth in iniquity, and in sin my mother conceived me." This simply means that my mother, as all mothers, was born with sin, and therefore I was born with a sinful nature also.

When a child is left alone with this sin nature and is not given proper instruction and correction, the parents can expect the result stated in Proverbs 29:15: "The rod and reproof give wisdom, but a child left to himself brings shame to his mother." A child not diverted from the original condition into which he was born will bring shame to both his mother and his father: "A foolish son is a grief to his father and bitterness to her who bore him" (Proverbs 17:25).

I'm afraid that parents often just endure their children for the 18 or 19 years they are in their care because it does take time and effort to give them the guidance and loving training that they all need. There is great danger ahead for the child who is allowed to just grow up without any training or discipline, and there will be great sorrow and heartache ahead for the parents of such a child. Every child has the potential of becoming a delinquent and even a criminal when he is left to his own ways without instruction and correction.

Desire Toward Good

Psalm 139:13-16 states: "You have formed my inward parts; You have covered me [woven me] in my mother's womb. I will praise You, for I am fearfully and wonderfully made; marvelous are Your works, and that my soul knows very well. My frame was not hidden from You when I was made in secret and skillfully wrought in the lowest parts of the earth [protected place]. Your eyes saw my substance, being yet unformed, and in Your book they all were written, the days fashioned for me, when as yet there were none of them."

God's plan for every new life began even before conception, but after conception the Creator guided the development and superintended the intricate design of each little person. Even before we were born He went so far as to list our members and what He had planned for us in the book of life (Psalm 139:13-16). Each one of us as developing little babies already had distinctive characteristics of our own that would later be revealed in the temperaments we would become.

All of this happened before we were even formed. God knew what He wanted us to be and what His plan was for our lives. It was never God's plan for a mother to deliberately end the life of a baby in her womb. This is clearly spelled out in Deuteronomy 30:19: "I have set before you life and death, blessing and cursing; therefore choose life." Every little preborn child should be granted the gift of becoming a completed person.

However, God also gave each of us a free will to choose evil or good, and the child that is not trained to choose good will undoubtedly choose evil. God knew what our natures would be and gave us many verses in the Bible to instruct us regarding evil and good. Romans 12:9b states, "Abhor what is evil. Cling to what is good"; verse 21 states, "Do not be overcome by evil, but overcome evil with good." Each child's desire for evil can partially be related to the weaknesses of his temperament, while his desire for good can be accomplished by the strengths of his temperament.

It is important for a parent to realize that it is natural for his child to have a desire for evil. The child is not just being obstinate and uncooperative but is following that natural desire to learn more about and to experience *evil*. There is a conflict going on within him because he has not yet been quickened or alerted to spiritual values.

Each child is born with very selfish desires and thinks only of his own wants. When denied his wants, he often reacts with rage and fits of anger. Can you see what a teenager or an adult would be like if left to those natural ego-centered desires? The parent who understands these natural tendencies will be more diligent in leading his child to know Christ and in teaching him to abhor evil and desire the good in life.

More parents need to comprehend the tremendous impact of teaching or neglecting to teach their children during the first eight years of their lives. Parents get only one chance; there are no dress rehearsals.

Parents need to conscientiously set goals for themselves in the development of their children. The very earliest sparks of interest in doing good need to be nurtured, protected, and trained. How beautiful it is to hear a young child, barely able to put a sentence together, quote "God is love" or "We love Him because He first loved us." If this tender young plant is not nurtured and watered, it will wither and die. There is no waiting until a more convenient time. Children will not wait for parents' schedules to improve while they build their careers or pursue their own interests. The training must be done while they are young, tender, and still trainable, because children just won't wait.

Children Won't Wait

There is a time to anticipate the baby's coming, a time to consult a doctor;

A time to plan a diet and exercise, a time to gather a layette.

There is a time to wonder at the ways of God, knowing this is the destiny for which I was crafted;

A time to dream of what this child may become,

A time to pray that God will teach me how to train this child which I bear.

A time to prepare myself that I might nurture his soul.

But soon there comes the time for birth,

For babies won't wait.

There is a time for night feedings, and colic and formulas.

There is a time for rocking and a time for walking the floor,

A time for patience and self-sacrifice,

A time to show him that his new world is a world of love and goodness and dependability.

There is a time to ponder what he is—not a pet or toy, but a person, an individual—a soul made in God's image.

There is a time to consider my stewardship. I cannot
   possess him.
He is not mine. I have been chosen to care for him, to
   love him, to enjoy him, to nurture him, and to an-
   swer to God.
I resolve to do my best for him,
For babies won't wait.
There is a time to hold him close and tell him the
   sweetest story ever told;
A time to show him God in earth and sky and flower,
   to teach him to wonder and reverence.
There is a time to leave the dishes, to swing him in
   the park,
To run a race, to draw a picture, to catch a butterfly, to
   give him happy comradeship.
There is a time to point the way, to teach his infant lips
   to pray,
To teach his heart to love God's Word, to love God's
   day.
For children won't wait.
There is a time to sing instead of grumble, to smile
   instead of frown,
To kiss away the tears and laugh at broken dishes.
A time to share with him my best in attitudes—a love
   of life, a love of God, a love of family.
There is a time to answer his questions, all his
   questions,
Because there may come a time when he will not want
   my answers.
There is a time to teach him so patiently to obey, to put
   his toys away.

There is a time to teach him the beauty of duty, the
habit of Bible study, the joy of worship at home, the
peace of prayer.

For children won't wait.

There is a time to watch him bravely go to school, to
miss him underfoot,

And to know that other minds have his attention, but
that I will be there to answer his call when he comes
home, and listen eagerly to the story of his day.

There is a time to teach him independence, responsibility, self-reliance,

To be firm but friendly, to discipline with love,

For soon, so soon, there will be a time to let him go, the
apron strings untied,

For children won't wait.

There is a time to treasure every fleeting minute of his
childhood.

Just eighteen precious years to inspire and train him.

I will not exchange this birthright for a mess of pottage
called social position, or business or professional
reputation, or a paycheck.

An hour of concern today may save years of heartache
tomorrow.

The house will wait, the dishes will wait, the new room
can wait,

But children won't wait.

There will be a time when there will be no slamming of
doors, no toys on the stairs, no childhood quarrels,
no fingerprints on the wallpaper.

Then may I look back with joy and not regret.

There will be a time to concentrate on serving outside my home:

On visiting the sick, the bereaved, the discouraged, the untaught;

To give myself to the "least of these."

There will be a time to look back and know that these years of motherhood were not wasted.

I pray there will be a time to see him an upright and honest man, loving God and serving all.

God, give me wisdom to see that today is my day with my children,

That there is no unimportant moment in their lives.

May I know that no other career is so precious,

No other work so rewarding,

No other task so urgent.

May I not defer it nor neglect it,

But by Thy Spirit accept it gladly and joyously, and by that grace realize

That the time is short and my time is now—

For children won't wait!

—Helen M. Young*

*Used by permission.

3

Do You Know Your Child?

Even though our children are part of our flesh and blood (if they are our natural children), we still have to work at getting to really know what makes them tick. And this is certainly true in cases of adoption or stepparenting. We are all made up of different and varying degrees of temperaments that cause us to be truly unique individuals. (We will study the specific temperaments in later chapters to help each parent understand his or her child more thoroughly.)

Insecurities can develop within a child without the parents being aware that it is even happening. For example, certain temperaments are more apt to feel left out than others. One young family of four had just arrived at Grandma's house for a visit. She welcomed them by taking the new six-week-old baby in her arms to love and admire her. After several moments of being ignored and feeling left out, the little four-year-old tugged at Grandma's skirt and said rather hesitantly, "Grandma, I'm here too!"

I'm sure most grandmas would not consciously do such a thing, but unfortunately many children feel left out because someone has not taken the time to see them for who they really are and to know their needs. The four-year-old needs to be known for himself; he wants the attention and affection equal to what is given the new baby. Even though youngsters may be different sexes and completely different temperaments, their need to be known will be similar.

Each Child Is Different

Regardless of how many children you have, each child will have different temperaments than his brothers and sisters. The genes that aid in determining the blend of temperaments are contributed from the two parents, four grandparents, and even eight great-grandparents.

After the birth of our first child, a gynecologist assured us that she was absolutely unique. He said that if we had 20 children, they would each be completely different, with varying personalities and different temperament blends. And each of our four children was in fact very different from the others, even though they all stemmed from the same two parents and the same four grandparents. By the time they had turned two years old, we had already begun to see definite differences and recognized a unique personality in each child. We learned quickly that we had to deal with each child in a different but fair manner.

Linda was our firstborn. She entered the world with a lovely, cheerful disposition. Since she was a curious child and very active, our quiet little household became a rumpus room of activity. After two years of living, it was easy to detect that she was a natural leader as she directed her dolls and her stuffed animals into obedience. Her ability to express herself with words developed at an early age, and she used it often. She responded very well to correction and discipline and had a sensitive heart for spiritual things.

As we got to know Linda better, we began to appreciate her thoughtful concern for the welfare of others, her leadership ability, and her keen sense for right and wrong. If we had not taken the time to really know her, these strengths could have been overlooked and never encouraged and developed. Linda was truly a delightful child to raise.

After two years Larry came along. He seemed to slip quietly into our family with not too much fanfare. Since he was quiet-natured and easily contented, he could amuse himself for long periods of time. And of course he had a sister to help entertain him. He did not often assert himself but was content to go along with his sister's wishes. At the age of two he would sit and study his playthings, seeming to be in deep thought as to how to create new ways of playing with old toys.

His pensive moments would be interspersed with moments of mischievousness, making him a lovable and interesting little package. He was a little more difficult to get to know because of his quiet manner, but he could ask the deepest questions and expect answers to them. How important it was for his proper development that we took the time to study and know him! Many fine qualities would otherwise have been overlooked and passed by. Inside the quiet child is often a reservoir of talent that needs to be let loose and properly directed.

Lee arrived three years after Larry. His entrance into the world was like an explosion. This boy was an adorable child, and loving him was like loving both a kitten and a lion at the same time. He could purr and roar with one breath. His complexity was a challenge to us, but still he entwined himself around our heartstrings with his tender, loving ways.

Before his second birthday we had already noticed two distinct characteristics: One was his strong will and unending determination, and the second was the gifted mind which God had given him. Taking the time to know Lee probably made the difference between his becoming a well-adjusted young man rather than a rebellious heartbreak to his parents.

As we got to recognize and know his mood changes, we were better able to help him because we were aware of his weaknesses. He tested our patience and our discipline, but he responded with a sensitive spirit and provided a lovable and challenging experience for us as parents.

Four years later our fourth child arrived in the form of a little girl named Lori. She was a happy, giggly, and bubbly baby. Her charisma was a beautiful blend with the temperaments of the other three. When conflicts would arise between the children, she was the peacemaker who would give in to restore tranquility and harmony. Her desire to please was so strong that she was rarely disobedient; on the few occasions when she was, there was little need for stern discipline. A disapproving look from Mom or Dad was about all that was necessary.

Her first two years of living revealed that the world was her stage and she was the star. In many ways it has been her cheerful approach to life that has woven the threads of warmth and close fellowship throughout our family. It was not too difficult to really know Lori because she was open and candid about everything. We had to learn quickly that, because of her active involvement with life, it was necessary for us to be able to rise and fall with her joys and sorrows.

All four children have made a definite impact on our lives, and they are loved and adored equally by us. But how different they are! Each one contributed individual talents and assets in making the family unity that we now enjoy. The varying joys and sorrows they created taught us to learn to cope with each child according to his own temperament. A supersensitive child cannot be dealt with in the same way as the child who is bullheaded and strong-willed. Nor can the fearful child be treated in the same way as the bold, aggressive child.

Knowing Each Child

To assist in the proper development and training of children, it is very helpful if, during each child's early years, the parents learn his temperament characteristics. The heart and center of the parent-child relationship is knowing and understanding each child.

My purpose in using these personal illustrations is to show how very different each child can be. Perhaps you will more quickly recognize and identify your own children's temperaments as you hear the stories of others. Perhaps God gave us a sample of each of the four temperaments so we could help other parents begin to know and understand their own children.

Note to single parents: This book is for you as well as the two-parent families. Even though I don't always single you out specifically, you are included every time I refer to parents, mothers, fathers, etc. The number of single-parent homes has increased dramatically since the first edition of this book was written, and now we cannot discuss families and raising children without including single parents as well. So please feel comfortable as you browse through these pages, for you are not forgotten!

4

Temperament Alert

I don't understand why Johnny acts like he does. He sure doesn't get it from his father or me!" These were the exact words of a frustrated mother who could not understand why her Johnny acted like he did. It would have helped if she realized that he acted as he did because of the combinations of genes received from his parents, grandparents, and even great-grandparents. The influence of this entire group of people contributes to the temperament of each child. Is it any wonder that some children act like their parents, others act more like their grandparents, and still others do not resemble either because they are a blend of several combinations of people?

My husband has written several books that give a very detailed presentation of the four basic temperaments, among them *Spirit-Controlled Temperament* and *Transformed Temperament* (Tyndale House Publishers). I have a newly revised and expanded edition of *Spirit-Controlled*

Woman (Harvest House Publishers) that is directed specifically toward women, and Tim has a newly revised and enlarged edition of *Understanding the Male Temperament* (Fleming H. Revell). I suggest that you refer to these writings for a complete study of the temperaments. However, in the pages that follow we will discuss the immature temperament traits as observed in children.

In preparation for writing this book I have had many discussions with mothers whose children were of various temperaments and ages. My two married daughters encouraged me by helping me observe their children and by arranging planning sessions for me with many of their friends.

One primary observation we have all made is that by the time a child is two to three years old, he has probably begun to fit into one or two temperament characteristics. Please remember that no one is a single temperament; we are all unique combinations of at least two and occasionally three temperaments. We will be discussing the child's immature characteristics, which are nonetheless the beginning resemblance of what he will become. Because we are dealing with immaturity, the child will not be locked into absolute temperament traits. At different stages of growth and development he will react with some degree of variance. Inhibitions may cause him to alter and subdue some of his basic traits, and environment can be a great influence on him while he is finding himself. He may even be affected by new motivations that will result in a temporary change of pattern.

But even though his ways may be unstable during these formative years, the majority of the time he will resemble the temperament he is becoming. The following four chapters will take a look at the childlike traits of the four basic temperaments: Sanguine, Choleric, Melancholic, and Phlegmatic. Then we will discuss the 12 blends of temperaments which reveal why each child can be so uniquely different.

5

The Talkative and Fun-Loving Sanguine

The little Sanguine can easily be recognized by his friendly and steady stream of talking. Nobody is a stranger—everyone is his best friend. Even before he learns to talk he can say so much with his cheerful disposition and devilish personality. His winning smile keeps him from many a scolding, and he may try to get through life by being Mr. Friendly. He is the child who sits in the seat of a grocery cart and rides through the grocery store asking everyone what their name is and where they live.

This temperament is the one that will stand out in a group of children by being the loudest and the most boisterous. He has a short interest span and will restlessly flit from stacking blocks to climbing on chairs, flipping the TV switches, or any other mischievous thing his mind happens to think of. The world is his stage and he will clown or show off to be the center of attention.

In little children we think this to be cute, but when they reach the junior age it seems disgusting. Yet they are the same temperament with the same traits, but with bigger bodies. Usually the Sanguine is a mimic, and you will see him acting like people he has been around. All children are pretenders, but the Sanguine will be able to pretend and get over it—a very normal and healthy characteristic.

One of our grandchildren is a lovable Sanguine. He has been the cause of some very tense moments for his grandmother, especially when he was a toddler. Sanguines are usually daredevils, climbers, act-now-and-think-later people. This little man was all of that. One day at my home I walked into the entry to see him climbing on the outside edge of a stair railing that had a drop of about 12 feet to a hard tile surface below. His little hands were hanging tightly to the railing while his toes were barely able to fit on the small area outside the railing. Just as he took his last step to the highest ledge, he turned to me with a winning smile. He was not yet two and was not talking much, but if he had been able, he probably would have said, "Hi, Grandma, look what I've done!"

There was no fear at that moment (except in *my* heart)—just smiles and joy at his accomplishment. The fear came when I told him he had to come down, and he could only get down the same way he got up. He cried every step down as I encouraged him and insisted he keep coming. Sanguines are very prone to act on impulse and then think later. I wish I could say he learned his lesson and never tried it again, but he had to try it several times more before he learned that I meant what I said about staying off the railing.

Now that the young climber has reached adulthood (which has surprised us all), he still enjoys a thrill-a-minute lifestyle. He will go through life with the cavalier attitude that life is here to enjoy and he will enjoy it.

One observation I have made is that this temperament seems to be eager to please. The little Sanguines in my life seem very willing to say "please" and "thank you." They fully intend to be obedient and to please, but they get swept away with curiosity or a change of environment. Although many times they may seem to be deliberately disobedient, they are probably just forgetting the past and becoming engulfed in the present moment. They easily forget the past punishments and don't consider the problems their disobedience may present.

Sanguines can be easy liars. They get caught up in bragging and exaggerating about themselves until their stories are no longer true. They also find it easy to test the rules. Repentance comes easy but is often short-lived.

Even when punished severely, Sanguines quickly change their moods and may be heard singing or whistling only moments later. Two little children were punished for outright disobedience and then sent to their individual rooms until they finished crying. The Choleric child must have stayed there for 15 or 20 minutes, all the time screaming and complaining loudly. The little Sanguine was over his sadness in 30 seconds and then dashed outside to play. Two minutes later he was on his swing sailing high into the sky and singing at the top of his lungs, "Jesus loves me, this I know." But even after the 20 minutes, when the Choleric came out of her room she was anything but happy. She drooped around and complained for at least an hour.

A Sanguine has a difficult time playing alone. He is so people-oriented that it is very important for him to have brothers, sisters, or neighbors to play with. He loves to share himself and his possessions to gain new friends, but his loving nature can change to immediate anger when something crosses him. The explosion may resemble a volcano erupting, but he will readily apologize and beg for forgiveness. He is the little child on the playground that cries, "I'm sorry, I didn't mean to!" His emotions are a combination of highs and lows, as shown by his laughter that is quickly changed to tears, and vice versa.

Because of his quick-changing moods, the Sanguine can readily adjust to disappointments and make the best of the situation. I watched a sanguine teenage girl go through a series of disappointments in her high school years that would have finished off any Melancholic. After each disappointment she hit an emotional low, but she came out of every experience with a beautiful, rejoicing spirit. She had parents who would not allow her to engage in self-pity but encouraged her to look for the things she could be thankful for. The danger for this temperament is that after a discouragement he may drift into a pattern of feeling sorry for himself and work himself into a state of depression.

The Sanguine could be a good student but rarely is because of his restlessness. He has the capabilities, but his undisciplined and weak-willed nature hinder his persistence in good study habits. He can overcome this deficiency if he is taught to discipline himself in all areas of life and to allow the Holy Spirit to make use of his great potential. Parents need to be aware of this weakness and to help him develop better work habits and learn how to plan his time.

This carefree, happy-go-lucky temperament will be difficult to recognize when he does not have the security of a loving and stable home. He needs to be loved and accepted by others, particularly his family. When his parents are quarrelsome and unhappy, then he reflects that spirit by becoming sullen and withdrawn. All Sanguines need to be loved, and when they do not find love at home they may look outside the family for this need to be filled. They have a need for instant gratification and have very little self-control.

Parents, be forewarned that teenage Sanguines need close supervision lest they fall into temptation. They are prone to be followers, and their peers can lead them into abuses that have major consequences. Their experimentation with drugs could be the result of running with peers who have encouraged this practice and give the Sanguines a sense of being accepted by the group. Be watchful of the kind of friends they have!

The Sanguine will also be responsive to spiritual things. He has a compassionate heart and responds to those who love him. When he hears that God loved him and that Jesus died for him, his tender Sanguine heart will respond readily. He may walk in and out of fellowship with Christ because he is a follower without strong convictions, but he is usually willing to repent and start over again. Most Sanguine children who are exposed to the gospel message receive Christ at an early age. But they need careful guidelines to direct them as they walk through their youthful years.

6

The Independent and Self-Sufficient Choleric

One of the earliest temperaments to discern in children is the Choleric. By two years of age he will have developed an independent spirit and will attempt to do things for himself that other children would not try until much later. This could include anything from feeding himself and tying his own shoes to riding a bicycle. The Choleric child is quite self-sufficient and rather insistent in climbing out of a stroller or walking through the shopping center unassisted.

Unlike the Phlegmatic, who will quietly and stubbornly disobey and do his own thing, the Choleric will loudly and angrily proclaim his disapproval and then proceed to demonstrate it to you. He is easily recognized by his strong will and determined spirit. However, this strong will need not be a hindrance to the spiritual growth of the child if the parent can bend that will at an early age.

Susanna Wesley, the mother of 19 children, once said, "The self-willed child must be broken and brought into subjection before he reaches two years of age." She must have found the key that works, because two of her sons shook the continents of Great Britain and North America with their ministry for God.

It is the *will* that must be broken and not the *spirit* of the choleric. The young person who has a strong will that is totally submitted to God will be greatly helped by this strength of character to stand against the temptations of youth. He has the potential to be a leader of great influence, for good or bad, rather than merely a follower.

The young Choleric, like the mature one, will be an active person and a strong leader. Our Choleric daughter was a dominant leader among the neighborhood children. Some of them were older than she was, yet she was not intimidated by their age. She could organize and lead the sandbox activity, the jumprope competition, or the family schedule for doing dishes. It was her natural gift that God had built into her. Had she not submitted her dominant spirit to the Lord to control and use for His glory, she could have turned into an abusive person and a poor marriage partner.

Today this young woman still has the gift of leadership, and she uses it by serving as California State Director of Concerned Women for America. But she also is a beautiful example of a Spirit-controlled wife who is submissive both to God and to her husband. The Lord has sharpened this gift in her but has smoothed off the rough edges, and He continues to put her in areas of leadership where she can be effective and pleasing to God. He wants her to use the gifts of her temperament; however, they must be controlled by the Holy Spirit to be truly effective.

One trait of this temperament that frequently surfaces is blunt, sarcastic speech. Because the Choleric is self-confident and not always concerned about pleasing people, he will speak what he thinks, even though it may be cutting or offensive. Little children are naturally honest and straightforward because they are uninhibited; however, the Choleric child is not only honest but almost brutal. He will test you to see how far you will let him go.

One of our grandchildren tested my authority one day by disobeying me and then announcing to me, "You're not my mother and I don't have to mind you!" I didn't take this personally or feel offended because I knew that this little Choleric was simply testing me, and I needed to prove to her that she *did* have to mind me when she was left in my care. Now, many years later, we are best friends and she has a beautiful witness in her life. But it took many confrontations and a consistent effort to break her stubborn will to accomplish this end result.

When two Choleric children play together, you can be sure there will be conflict almost immediately. Since this temperament has to be the boss of the group, and there is usually room for only one boss, Cholerics tend to gravitate to the other temperaments whom they can dominate.

One day while entertaining my grandchildren during the Christmas holidays, I observed how different temperaments responded to a similar situation. Our Christmas tree had a special hanging ornament that was of sentimental value to me, and I did not want the children playing with it. When I realized it was within their reach and all three of them were attracted to it, I moved it higher on the tree and offered them a less valuable object to play with.

The Sanguine child seemed just as interested in the new object and couldn't have cared less about the more valuable one. The Phlegmatic studied it carefully and then stood back to see what the other children were going to do. Not the Choleric! That child protested loudly that she didn't like the substitute ornament and wanted the first one. I explained that this was a special one that was to be looked at but not touched and that the second ornament was one they could handle and admire. In a few moments this determined child had pushed a chair up to the tree, and I caught her just as her hand was about to grasp the ornament. After dealing with the situation and the disobedience, I removed the temptation and placed the ornament on a high shelf in the closet until the children had left.

Much later I entered the room to find that this same child had dragged a chair across the room and was hanging by her fingertips trying to reach the forbidden ornament! Such determination becomes an admirable characteristic only when it can be submitted to authority and directed toward goals that are productive and beneficial.

The Choleric child needs to have definite areas of responsibility and leadership. It is very necessary for him to develop this natural-born characteristic under the watchful eye and loving direction of his parents. The degree of responsibility should increase with the age and development of the child. The Choleric has an active mind which can best be controlled and directed by putting him in charge of responsible areas.

This temperament thrives on activity that is productive. I have seen a teenage Choleric very successfully take the full responsibility and leadership of a high school banquet. He accepted the challenge and rose to the occasion. With committees selected and organized, he proceeded to move at top speed. Unfortunately, the committee members were not all Cholerics and did not have the same drive and determination that he did. The other temperaments had difficulty working with this leader because he had a tendency to be a hard driver and unreasonable with his demands. When the others fell short, the young Choleric strongly reprimanded them and expressed his feelings about their inadequacy, then picked up their unfinished load and completed the project himself.

However, in spite of how he accomplished his goal, the end result was very successful. What he needed to learn was how to lead and motivate other temperaments to cooperate and carry their share of the load. This could only come from experience and maturity.

Unlike the Sanguine's ability to lie to improve his own ego, the Choleric will exercise his independence and lie to get around the rules. He does not like being told no, so he learns to sidestep the no by lying. Repentance is not a natural thing for him, and it will be difficult for him to admit he has done any wrong.

When it comes to trying drugs, he is more prone to stand against his peers and tell them they are crazy for getting involved. However, if he ever does try drugs, he will want to lead his friends to try them also.

It is important to teach Cholerics about virtue and abstinence early in life. Then they can lead the cause of promoting abstinence with their peers. But if they become sexually active before they learn about abstaining from sex until marriage, they have the potential of being aggressively promiscuous.

The Choleric child should be led to the Lord by the time he is 12 years old because the chances of a later decision for Christ become very slim. However, he is the most responsive to spiritual things before that time. This is probably because of his natural characteristic to be self-confident and self-sufficient. After his junior years, his confidence grows with maturity and he has difficulty feeling the need for a heavenly Father. His natural characteristic is to be so independent that he doesn't need the support of others. So, it becomes difficult for him to depend on the Holy Spirit for help and guidance. His motto is "I can do it myself," when he really needs the Lord's help.

7

The Gifted and Faithful Melancholic

The Melancholic temperament can be the most gifted and have the deepest depression all wrapped up in one little package. God has endowed him with a brilliant mind and the ability to be a deep and creative thinker. His sensitive, artistic nature is often affected by his attitude toward others or what he thinks their attitudes toward him might be. It is easy for him to have his feelings hurt and to feel inferior, believing that others do not like him.

Even though the Melancholic may possess the greatest talents of any of the temperaments, he often suffers under the delusion of an inferiority complex. Parents of a Melancholic child should be especially considerate of this problem. Because of his sensitive nature and his tendency toward perfection, he cannot handle criticism and will sink deeper into an inferior state.

A little two-year-old is capable of showing his temperament traits by switching from one mood to another without too much cause. The extremity of his mood swings will be determined by his secondary temperament, which will be discussed in a later chapter. He can sit sullen and quiet, enjoying his loneliness, and then later become an outgoing, aggressive actor much like a Sanguine.

It is possible that the Melancholic will learn to escape reality by living in a make-believe, fantasy world. The wise parents will continually bring him back to face reality and any consequences that accompany it. When little Johnny repeatedly says, "I didn't do it—Tommy did," and Tommy is an imaginary friend, then Johnny needs to learn that he cannot hide behind Tommy. He needs to face the reality of confessing "I did it." Too many Johnnys have grown up to continually blame others for their mistakes or disobedience instead of admitting their own wrongdoing, confessing it, and facing the consequences.

This child has such great potential, but he needs so much help and understanding! When left to his own ways he will no doubt grow up to become a gloomy, pessimistic, self-pitying individual. Fortunate is the child who has parents who will teach him how to have joy and thankfulness instead of gloom, a wholesome and positive attitude instead of a negative attitude, and a spirit of praise instead of self-pity.

We watched a Melancholic junior boy who had most of the weaknesses of this temperament develop into a whiner with a critical spirit. One day his parents realized something had to be done, so they prayerfully approached him and openly discussed the problem. It was their decision, in an effort to help him, that they would not approve of him speaking negatively or critically again. When he did, it would be brought to his attention and he would have to replace it with a positive and thankful statement before he could enter the conversation again. They wanted him to learn to be silent if he could not say something good and praiseworthy about a subject. It has been interesting to watch this boy after about eight or ten years. He has a new spirit and seems much happier with himself because of it.

A friend of mine received several letters from her daughter, who was away for a few weeks over the summer. My friend shared the letters with me, and they were filled with nothing but problems her daughter had been faced with, including some real disappointments. I concluded that the girl was having a terrible time and that every possible difficulty was happening to her. When she returned we were able to spend some time together, and I commented how sorry I was that her summer experience had been such a disastrous one. She was stunned by my reaction and quickly informed me that she had had the time of her life. Yet in her letters she had dwelt on just the problems and never mentioned the great time she was having.

Negativism is a habit pattern that children can easily slip into, and it is best broken when they are still young and pliable and able to change.

Even though the Melancholic is the most gifted, he will be the last one to recognize it. He has a poor self-image and entertains many feelings of failure and inability. Parents should start when he is very young to help him see what God has given him in talents and abilities and then learn to thank God for them.

Parents need to be on the alert and watchful for any radical changes in his grades at school. It could be the first indicator that this normally good student is experimenting with drugs. Often the Melancholic finds comfort in smoking pot because he thinks it helps him overcome his depressive moods. And it may do so temporarily, but the long-range result could be devastating. Children are getting involved with drugs at an earlier age than ever before, so do not be naive as a parent. Watch for any signs of irregularities. Visit your children's bedrooms and keep your eyes open. Be on the lookout for any changes in his study habits or his grades.

The Melancholic child sets very high goals for himself, and when they are not reached he gets very depressed. When he doesn't receive the highest grade on a test he is sure he is failing the course and becomes very discouraged. He is overly conscientious; everything has to be nearly perfect. This tendency leads him to produce very excellent term papers or reports that are both attractive and well-written.

My daughter went through school with a lovely Melancholic girlfriend. This girl had many of the strengths of her temperament, and because of her spiritual growth, the weaknesses were not too pronounced. These girls were the very best of friends through the elementary grades, junior high, and high school. Other girlfriends would come and go with each passing year, but these two remained fast, loyal friends.

I watched while their friendship was tested time and time again, and even though it seemed rocky for awhile, they would emerge faithful, loyal friends. One of the admirable characteristics of the Melancholic is that he is such a faithful friend. Even today, though the girls are married and are living in different cities with their husbands and children, their friendship has remained steadfast and true. We feel fortunate that our daughter has such a beautiful and loyal friend!

The Melancholic young person may be the last one in the family to marry, regardless of whether he is male or female. He will have difficulty finding someone to meet up to his perfectionist and idealistic standards for a life partner. Some Melancholics have been known to back out of the wedding at the last moment because they got cold feet when they realized that their new partner was not perfect. Of course it is far better that he change his mind before the wedding than after, but sometimes it is just the fear of making such a weighty decision that keeps him from the marriage altar. However, this delay in marriage does not necessarily mean he has abstained from sex. The Melancholic person does crave love. Sometimes a teenage boy or girl will trade his or her virtue for intimacy, particularly if there has been a lack of love from a parent.

After discussing Melancholic children with many different mothers, I have drawn one strong conclusion: Parents of Melancholic children rarely agree on how to raise them. Many have told me that the most severe clashes in their marriage regarding raising children were on how to discipline their Melancholic child.

One mother told me that, after 22 years of a good, solid marriage, she and her husband developed a critical and antagonistic spirit toward each other over their differences regarding their Melancholic child. She accused him of being too harsh and insensitive toward this tender child, and he felt she was ruining the child by being overprotective.

Every time he attempted to discipline the child he felt she was disapproving, and, according to her own story, she probably was.

In other instances the mother is overly harsh and the father is the protector. Most likely the parent with the more extroverted temperament will be accused of being hard and insensitive to the Melancholic. The introvert will tend to draw him under a protective wing.

The Melancholic has the potential to be outstanding with his God-given gifts and creativity and to excel among his peers. But he also has the capability to sink below his companions with his strong feelings of inferiority and pessimism. In short, the Melancholic is rarely an average child because he has the greatest strengths and also the most devastating weaknesses. Yet with the Lord's help he can accomplish great things in his lifetime.

8

The Patient and Easygoing Phlegmatic

The easiest child to raise may be the one who has a predominantly Phlegmatic temperament, simply because he is naturally quiet, easygoing, and calm. This baby is usually the contented one and will be happy just lying in the crib looking at the four corners of the ceiling. Because he is not demanding of a mother's time and attention, she may be guilty of taking advantage of his calmness by not spending the time that he needs to cuddle and play with him.

As he grows from infancy to young childhood, the Phlegmatic may be slow at learning to talk, not because he lacks intelligence but because he is not too expressive anyway and is just being a spectator of life. This is especially true if he thinks someone else will do the talking for him. His motto is, "Why overexert myself?" One day I asked my little Phlegmatic grandson what his dog's name was.

By the time he had his lips in position to answer, his Choleric sister had already responded for him and was off to handle another situation.

He is usually a slow eater and may enjoy just rearranging the food on his plate. Unlike the Sanguine, who lives to eat (if he can be silent long enough), the Phlegmatic may not put that much importance on eating unless it is a favorite food he really enjoys.

One parent told me of her Phlegmatic child who was slowly enjoying his dinner. The dessert had been set at each plate on the table at the beginning of the meal. The little Phlegmatic had diddle-daddled along through the whole meal and, as usual, was the last one at the table still eating. But he finally finished his meal and, thinking he was through, he left the table. It was not until the next day that he remembered he had not eaten his dessert, though it had not been left on the table. His Sanguine brother confessed that he had taken the dessert when his brother was not looking and, after waiting so long for him to notice it was gone, finally decided to eat it himself. That is enough to make a slow "Phleg" eat like a hungry Sanguine!

Because this temperament is an introvert, his weaknesses may not show too readily, particularly when he is young. Since his greatest problem is a lack of motivation, he can skirt around this during his younger years. You may notice his attempts to ignore your instructions to put away his toys, to hang up his clothes, or to finish taking out the trash.

Like other children, the Phlegmatic will lie to get out of a mess he is in, but most often he will back away from a situation to protect his own hide. All of the temperaments need to be taught that honesty in all things is the only way to live.

Another weakness the Phlegmatic is bothered with is his stinginess or selfishness. Most young children have a problem with sharing their belongings with other children, but the Phlegmatic tends not to outgrow this. As a young child, when other temperaments are beginning to be generous and to share, he can be seen gathering his things under his arms for protection and control.

I was a guest in a certain home where there were three children, ages three, four and six. Other friends, who had two more children around the same ages, were expected to arrive. The three children were happily playing together with a building set on the family room floor when the doorbell rang. The parents announced that the friends had arrived with the two other children. I observed the three-year-old Sanguine gather as many toys in her two hands as she could hold and rush to the door to share them with the visiting children. Meanwhile the four-year-old Phlegmatic began to scoop the remaining toys around him so he could stuff them into his pockets and under his sweatshirt. By the time the guests had entered the room, he was standing there with pockets bulging, sweatshirt sagging, and looking very much like an overstuffed teddy bear. He was not about to share with these intruders!

The Phlegmatic child will be the easiest of the temperaments to take into a restaurant for a meal. Even though he may not engage in eating too well, he will entertain himself by watching the activity going on around him. The same is true when taking him into a church service. (All churches do not have nurseries for the youngsters.) I remember sitting in the back during a particular service and noticing two young children sitting with their parents in front of me. One child, who was obviously Choleric and Sanguine, had her parents sitting on the edge of the pew while she demanded their full attention during the service. Finally, in desperation, the mother picked up the child and walked out the door. Just as she passed by, I caught a sparkling gleam in the child's eye that said loud and clear, "Finally, she's taking me out!"

On the same pew sat another couple with a child about the same age and even the same sex. This little girl was sitting on her daddy's lap deeply engrossed in a baby's hairbrush. She was carefully examining every bristle on the brush and then would gently stroke her hair from every angle. Her parents were listening intently to the sermon and paid little attention to the child. Why the vast difference? One child was definitely a quiet, calm Phlegmatic while the other was an active, determined Choleric.

One of the greatest joys a Phlegmatic can have is successfully teasing. Teasing can be a pleasant pastime or it can be his way of getting back at a person who annoys him. His strategy is to tease long enough so that the person who has annoyed him will eventually blow up or lose control. This is especially true where his siblings are concerned. They also enjoy teasing just for the sake of teasing.

Our Phlegmatic son knew that our daughter scared very easily. Nothing delighted him more than to slip quietly into the basement laundry room where his sister would not hear him because of the noise from the washer and dryer. He would get right behind her and then give off a loud yell. She would nearly jump out of her skin and many times broke into tears just from fright. They laugh about it today, but years ago his teasing was a real trauma in our daughter's life.

Because the Phlegmatic is easily led by his peers, the wise parent will be very aware who his friends are, especially as he approaches the teen years. Peer pressure may be stronger than the fear of the risks of such things as smoking pot, sampling different drugs, or having sex. All of what you may have taught him could be temporarily set aside in order to be accepted by his peers.

As this temperament becomes a teenager, he may want to draw away from his church peer group and activities that would benefit him socially and spiritually. He needs to be encouraged to be a participant and not just a spectator. The right kinds of friends are very important in keeping him on the right path. He will have much to offer society but will probably need a gentle push from time to time to get involved and stay involved.

It is very important that the Phlegmatic learn responsibility during his growing years so that he can successfully handle his freedom when he reaches adulthood. This is a potentially great temperament if he has learned self-motivation and self-discipline.

9

Twelve Blends of Children's Temperaments

After reading the previous chapters introducing the four basic temperaments you may find it somewhat difficult to identify your children's temperaments. This is because no person exactly fits the description of one temperament only; we are all a blend of at least two. Therefore this may be the most important chapter of all because it will discuss the 12 most common blends of the temperaments. Most parents find it easier to identify their children as one of the 12 blends than as one of the four basic temperaments.

Certainly all blends are not found in the same proportion. A child who is 75 percent Sanguine and 25 percent Choleric (we call him "SanChlor") will be quite different from the child who is 80 percent Choleric and 20 percent Sanguine ("ChlorSan"). In breaking down the temperaments on the following pages, I have used the proportions of 60 percent for the primary temperament and 40 percent for the secondary. In a single chapter I could not possibly list all the combinations of percentages within the 12 blends of temperaments, but a brief discussion of the 60/40 percent combinations will demonstrate the variety in the basic trends. This information should help you make any further breakdown of the proportions for yourself.

SanChlor

Since both of these temperaments are outgoing by themselves, they result in a very strong extrovert when blended. The enthusiasm of the Sanguine combined with the drive and character of the Choleric creates a more productive person than one who is totally Sanguine. The influence of the Choleric gives him a bit more determination than he would normally have. Whatever the SanChlor person does, he must have activity and excitement. If there is none, he will persist until he gets it going.

He loves sports but must be a participant, not an observer. If he isn't fortunate enough to be on the team, he will certainly be the loudest spectator in the stand. The SanChlor girl will often release her bundle of enthusiasm by being a cheerleader during the sport season, or being a leader of whatever she is involved with.

The SanChlor is extremely talkative and usually says and tells more than he ought—not only about himself but sometimes about his parents or friends. By his persistent talking he usually reveals his weak points and would be better off to say less. In school he will tell all that happens at home. Is it any wonder that the first time the San-

Chlor's parents meet his schoolteacher she looks at them like they might have two heads?

He usually speaks before he thinks, and, regardless of the subject, he speaks as an authority. This uninhibited child has a giant ego; therefore he does not wear well over a long period of time with members of his peer group. If he senses the other children resisting him, he will come on stronger, causing them to resist him even more. He is either the lovable, fun-loving member in his group, or, when he feels threatened, he will become obnoxious and pushy to get his way.

Anger is one of the major problems with which the SanChlor has to cope. When he has been crossed, his anger comes to the top immediately and he explodes all over everyone. It is easy to tell when he is being disrespect-ful—his mouth gives him away.

Although the SanChlor repents easily, he needs to be taught that he cannot defy his parents one minute to "get it off his chest," then apologize quickly the next minute to avoid the deserved punishment. He is a natural "con artist" who can go from anger to tears of repentance within four seconds. He needs to learn that a quick and easy repentance is not the same as a positive change in behavior.

When punishment is needed for a SanChlor, you will find that sitting in his room is often more effective than spanking. Because he is so restless, he would much rather get spanked quickly to get it over with so he can be on his way out the door.

The parents of the SanChlor need to help the child face his own wrong deeds and to teach him to take full re-sponsibility for his mistakes and sins. It is not always someone else's fault. He needs to learn that consideration for others must come before his own interests or goals and that circumstances in life are not always going to center around him. His anger usually stems from not getting his own way and can best be helped by not giving in to him or catering to his temper fits. From earliest childhood his parents need to help him develop habits of consistency, persistence, and self-discipline. Otherwise he will dissipate his many natural capabilities as he grows up.

Probably his greatest need is learning to finish what he starts. The Sanguine has the ability to start more things than he could ever finish. Having a portion of Choleric helps the SanChlor in this area, but he still needs to avoid taking on more than he can complete. Many a Sanguine gets excited about Boy Scouts just long enough to get his uniform, but when he has to work for merit badges, he loses interest.

Training in a SanChlor's discipline should begin at an early age. When he gets out a box of toys, he should not be permitted to leave them to play with something else before cleaning up the first mess. The parent will probably have to assist in this during the early years, but the child should at least be making a feeble attempt to help. Far more important than his helping to keep the house in order is your task of building character in the child and developing his much-needed art of self-discipline.

SanMel

The SanMel is highly emotional and fluctuates drastically between a flood of tears and hysterical laughter. He will both laugh and weep with his friends, depending upon the situation. In fact, he can be weeping one minute and then, for no apparent reason, begin laughing at himself, or vice versa. These children genuinely feel the hurt of others; they show real sorrow at the death of a pet or any animal.

They are very apt to be involved in acting, public speaking, or music. Because they are people-oriented, they will most likely participate in activities that give them an audience. One little SanMel girl was so desirous to perform that she developed a stage and props in the garage for her weekly performances. Sanguine children are born actors looking for a stage on which to perform.

Both Sanguines and Melancholics are dreamers, and as long as the Sanguine force predominates, his dreams will be positive, in full color, and with stereophonic sound. But when the Melancholic influence suggests a negative train of thought, his dreams return to black and white and begin to tumble; he starts to feel that he isn't capable of doing anything well and his self-image suffers. His moods may vary from exuberant highs to depressing lows.

The Sanguine has a problem with temper and the Melancholic with fear; therefore the SanMel is usually confronted with both fear and temper problems. This produces insecurity, so he needs to be surrounded by people who love him and accept him as he is. It is so important to him to be well thought of by others. He often needs to be reassured of parental love and approval.

This temperament has an esthetic nature and should be exposed to music lessons at a young age. Many of these children have started lessons and then talked their parents into letting them stop after a short while, only to regret it when they became older. Of all the temperament blends, SanMel is most apt to be an uninhibited performer with a natural enjoyment of music. Encouragement and discipline to keep up his lessons while young will provide him with opportunities to help others and to serve the Lord later in life, including the development of self-discipline. The SanMel, who often has many capabilities and talents, may never reach his potential because his parents failed to teach him the importance of self-discipline needed to reach a goal. He needs to work at becoming an achiever.

These children are prone to be fantastic fibbers. They are not satisfied with telling little "white lies." When they lie, the stories are usually so outlandish that they are obviously not the truth—like the little boy who told his mother that he didn't break the window when in fact he was the only one outside and had a bat in his hand. He also has the ability to be a "snow artist" and talk his way out of anything, especially in the face of punishment. This is the child who nervously tries to talk himself out of a spanking just before the paddle comes down on the designated place; he is quite capable at making a parent feel guilty for administering the spanking he earned.

The SanMel child will be socially conscious and an activist. He will be well-liked by friends and less obnoxious than the SanChlor. However, he is more of a perfectionist than the SanChlor and may alienate others by his verbal criticism of them. He needs to develop an understanding of and compassion for people less capable than himself. He often has a quick, retentive mind that needs to be taught self-discipline during his early years.

When this child has been taught proper self-discipline, he can develop into a real disciple for Jesus Christ because he has a genuine sensitivity toward spiritual things that usually reveals itself early in a Christian home. He may best excel in the fields of social science, math, science, or music, if he has learned to be an achiever and not a quitter.

SanPhleg

The most enjoyable children to raise can be the SanPhlegs when they aren't permitted to indulge their weaknesses. They are lovable, affectionate, happy little busybodies that rarely cause trouble. Like other Sanguines, they want what they want—right now—but they don't get quite as upset if they can't have it. Their interest span is extremely short-lived, and they are easily distracted by sounds or move-ment, particularly if it suggests people or activity. They are animal lovers and usually want to sleep with their pets. One two-year-old SanPhleg who saw tears running down the face of a family friend climbed up in her lap and said, "Aunt Shirley, let me kiss your tears away," and then pro-ceeded to try. They just naturally love people of any age.

The SanPhleg combines the uninhibited extroversion of the Sanguine and the witty good humor of the Phleg-matic, so he is usually very funny and delights in making others laugh. One salesman said after fitting clothes on a little five-year-old, "I'll bet you get a lot of laughs out of this kid." And usually you do if you give him lots of love.

Although he is a lovable type, the SanPhleg is not per-fect. Despite his natural charm and people-loving ways, the Sanguine lack of discipline and the Phlegmatic lack of motivation may frequently prove to be his undoing in life. If you have one of these fun-loving children, don't let his charisma and "big liquid eyes" blind you to the need to start teaching him early that he cannot be a quitter.

No one can leave his room in a greater disaster than the SanPhleg. One such teenager's father came in to awaken her one morning and found that the clothes she had worn the night before to a party were lying right where she had stepped out of them. In rage, he jerked her closet open to find 38 items of clothing lying on the floor. He actually counted them. Of all children, SanPhlegs are the least likely to plan for the future or worry about the past. In fact, they have a difficult time even remembering the past. You will soon discover that this child has to be punished repeatedly for the same thing.

Good study habits do not come easy for SanPhlegs, nor do good devotional practices. They mean well and often make loud public commitments to do better, but they seldom carry through unless their parents have used the first five years of life to teach them discipline and self-control. If they have a teacher they particularly enjoy, they may do well in that class but poorly in others. A SanPhleg child will do better to study in a room without wall pictures or anything else to distract him. Otherwise he will not be able to concentrate.

A high percentage of Sanguine children have a weight problem, and SanPhlegs probably have it more than any other. They have usually transformed their good physique at birth into a roly-poly body at ten and can anticipate a 2-to-5-percent increase every year thereafter unless their parents help them learn to eat properly and give them sufficient exercise.

Some children and their parents use the excuse that she or he "has a tendency to gain weight" or "they don't burn their calories off as fast as other children." There may be some truth to this claim, but more often the truth is that the children have poor eating habits—eating too fast, eating wrong foods, and eating between meals. Parents can help by trying to teach their children early in life to enjoy fruits and vegetables, to limit their sugar consumption, and to eliminate after-school and bedtime snacks. And by all means, candy, pop, and ice cream should be kept to a minimum.

SanPhlegs often have an insatiable sweet tooth. It is easier to curb this problem when they are little than when they are older. Recently we were in a missionary's home where their delightful SanPhleg ten-year-old won my heart. When his mother wasn't looking, I saw him "stuffing his face" from the candy dish—and he already carried about 15 pounds of excess fat. This is a common practice among SanPhlegs if not carefully controlled.

Weight control, unless some organic problem is involved, is a self-control and self-discipline problem. Instead of verbalizing discontent about the fact that a child is obese, his parents should help him to control his appetite so that he will learn self-control in other areas of life as well. We have seen SanPhlegs whose entire lives were transformed into a productive pattern once they conquered their weight problem.

The biggest difficulty in helping your child to gain control of his weight is that you have to set a good example or all your training will fail. One brokenhearted mother, 65 pounds overweight, recognized her bad eating habits in the lifestyle of her obese seven-year-old. She was frightened at the prospect of the fulfillment of the old adage "like mother, like daughter." It is important to practice what we preach!

ChlorSan

The 60 percent Choleric and 40 percent Sanguine child is not hard to spot. He is an extrovert, though not as extreme as his SanChlor counterpart. But he is a supreme activist and you know he is around! Don't be confused by the activity patterns of these first four temperament blends during the first years of life—they are all active children. The thing that distinguishes the ChlorSan is his determination, strong will (in some cases bullheadedness), independence, self-sufficiency, and hyperactivity. He usually has only two speeds: Wide open and sound asleep.

If very early you start bending that strong will to submit to your loving but firm authority and teach him to respect others, he will become a more enjoyable child. He has enough charm to sell most anything he sets his mind to—particularly his parents (if he can) on why he should have his own way. Be sure of this: He is out to have his own way and he can be impishly clever in his efforts to obtain it. It is not uncommon for him to start with charm and end up with temper if the charm doesn't work.

ChlorSans are good talkers, and early in life they will argue with their parents. In fact, they can't resist the temptation to get in the last word, and this will often be the cause for many of their punishments. Their tendency to justify their actions (whether right or wrong) provides them a ready answer as to why they should break the rules or why the rules should not apply to them.

In school, the ChlorSan is generally a sports lover who has to be a participant. If he is not fortunate enough to make the team, he can usually be found on the sidelines throwing a football—rarely is he a good spectator in youth. He loves competition and enjoys being at the center of the action. One of his youthful problems is getting home on time. He would rather be punished for being late (if he can't talk you out of it) than leave the ballpark early. He is a gifted debater and very argumentative, and this usually shows up by the time he can put three words together.

One of the ChlorSan's traits is being very opinionated and tending to declare himself before weighing the facts and then stubbornly trying to argue his way out of everything. He usually has a fiery temper, and both boys and girls who are ChlorSans will not hesitate to get into a fight. A fourth-grade ChlorSan moved to a new school where the class bully challenged him to a fight. Evenly matched, they both got so tired they had to quit with the promise to resume the next night. That went on for five nights in a row. Finally the two ChlorSans became the best of friends.

The ChlorSan is not often interested in studies but pursues more active interests. He loves to do projects that he can be in charge of and likes to be a director of other people. He needs to be guided to use his strong will to control his temper, speak respectfully, stop interrupting others, do his homework and chores, be considerate of the less powerful personalities, and avoid the use of sarcasm. He is the most affectionate of the three Choleric blends, but even he rations kisses as if they are scarce.

It is extremely important that you lead the ChlorSan to Christ and teach him the importance of being obedient to God early in life. All children should memorize Scripture in their third- to sixth-grade years, when their minds are highly impressionable, but the ChlorSan particularly needs to fortify his mind for the rebellious years ahead, when he is prone to do his own thing instead of the will of God.

ChlorMel

The ChlorMel child is not only active and productive, but often possesses a razor-sharp mind. Mothers are frequently disappointed that he is not loving, but instead is so independent that he only dispenses affection when he is in the mood. Fathers are frequently unprepared to be rejected by their little ChlorMel daughters and may tend to withdraw from them emotionally. It would be better for the parent to accept the child and his sparse expressions of affection on the child's terms, being careful to always return his love when he is in the mood. These children can learn to love, but it takes time.

ChlorMels can also be angry, willful, sassy, and sarcastic. They combine the hard-to-please traits of the Choleric and the perfectionism of the Melancholic. Their mouth is a dead giveaway when they are rebellious and they need to learn to use it kindly. Proverbs 13:3 says, "He who guards his mouth preserves his life, but he who opens wide his lips shall have destruction." It takes persistent training to teach ChlorMels to say "please" and "thank you." Even though in today's society these expressions are not commonly used among our youth, they are still a great asset in developing the character traits of thankfulness and appreciation.

No temperament blend can be more independent than the ChlorMel. I saw a two-year-old refuse her grandfather's offer to tie her shoes by saying, "I can do it myself!" In spite of the fact that she didn't know how, she was determined to try. In school the ChlorMel usually does well if taught good study habits and encouraged to balance his insatiable appetite for sports or outside activities against his need to study.

This child will usually come to a place in his life when he will try to refuse to go to church. The wise parent will be persistent and not cave in to the child's rebellious nature. If the parent just rolls over and lets the child have his way, then it won't be long before the next problem will be the choice of friends outside the church that could lead him to a path of destruction.

The secret thought life of a ChlorMel can be very dangerous. He is prone to be an angry child and, together with the revenge and self-persecution tendencies of the Melancholic, will exaggerate hurts, insults, or problems. Raising a ChlorMel can be a challenging experience, for it is never dull. If the parent who is the same sex as the child takes the time to develop a bonding relationship, the ChlorMel will do very well in life provided his strong will and determination are guided toward the control of his tongue, anger, and sarcastic attitude.

ChlorPhleg

The ChlorPhleg is an interesting combination of the hot and cool, providing a moderate temperament for this child. He is the least outgoing of the extroverts and is less likely to go off half-cocked in the wrong direction, for he is more deliberate and organized in everything he does. Once he sets out on a plan, he determinedly follows it through. It is not difficult to guide this child into good character traits at an early age. He is usually dependable and hardworking and can be an ideal child to raise if he does not develop an attitude of slow-burning inner animosity.

This child provides an interesting combination of the Choleric bullheaded determination and the Phlegmatic stubbornness. Consequently, it is difficult to get him to change his mind once it is made up. Like the other two Cholerics, it is very hard for him to admit when he is wrong, and repentance does not come easy for him. In sports it is hard for him to accept a penalty call by the coach (the coach must be wrong). In the classroom, the teacher who disciplines a ChlorPhleg is mistaken in the child's mind.

As a child he must not only be taught to bear the responsibility for his own mistakes, but also to apologize when he has made one. He is a master at getting other children into trouble without implicating himself. Although he is less likely to verbally explode at others and sarcastically cut them to ribbons than the other Cholerics, he is more apt to use his Phlegmatic humor to disguise it cleverly. He or she can be the nicest little troublemaker on the block.

Like all those with a predominantly Choleric temperament, he should be led to Christ before his twelfth birthday or he may never show an interest in spiritual things. As he gets older he becomes more set in his determination and stubbornness if not influenced by the power of the Holy Spirit in his life. ChlorPhleg children need lots of love and consistent discipline in the home, and they need parents who set a good example before them.

MelSan

The first six blends we have examined are predominantly extroverts. Now we shall turn to the more introverted temperaments. You can expect to recognize some similarities between them, except that some of their traits will be reversed.

No child is a greater bundle of emotions than the MelSan. He has the capability of going from laughter one moment to sobbing the next. He is naturally insecure and fear-prone and has an exaggerated guilt complex, so he needs an excessive amount of love and reassurance.

MelSan children are frequently gifted in creativity, art, music, science, or all of these. Strangely enough, they usually have a real problem with self-acceptance in spite of their many talents. If they are subjected to criticism or rejection, it is not uncommon for them to waste their amazing potential. Self-pity is a very dangerous thinking pattern to which a MelSan is vulnerable even to the point of being convinced his parents love his brothers and sisters more than they do him.

A MelSan child is not easy to raise because a parent may often be aware of the child's internal displeasure and criticism even if it is not verbalized. You need to remind yourself that he is usually just as critical of himself as he is of others. One thing he should learn early is that griping and criticism are not acceptable in your home. Be careful that you practice what you preach to him in this area. He has a keen sensitivity to spiritual things, so if his parents teach him in early childhood to refrain from negative thought patterns, to dwell on those things that are praiseworthy, and to reject the temptation to be critical, this can transform his personality, moodiness, and mental attitude.

Unless gifted in athletics, the MelSan may require more than the usual amount of help in learning sport skills. But don't be dismayed if you find that proper co-ordination for sporting activities is very difficult for your child. You may discover that your son or daughter has a natural bent toward art or music. If so, it would be wise to get special instruction to help him or her excel, both for his own self-acceptance and so that God can make better use of his talents.

This child may tend to be antisocial and must be encouraged to make and keep friends. You should particularly seek to get him into group activities—church groups, chorus, band, or team sports. Don't be surprised if he comes home and says, "I don't have any friends. Nobody likes me." He is a natural Charlie Brown type who needs to be taught to play with other children, even if he says he doesn't want to. If you have a MelSan, think of him as a diamond in the rough given to you by God to shape and to polish. Start early in being consistent, understanding, and loving, and you will later see him "shine as the stars," for he has a great capacity to serve God.

MelChlor

The MelChlor boy or girl is like clay in the potter's hands. The parent can mold him into a positive and capable person or accentuate his negative feelings until his above-average potential is neutralized. As young children

MelChlors are often fussier than other temperaments, very demanding and tending to be possessive clingers. It is not uncommon for them to be whiny, selfish, and hard to get along with. Consequently, they may not on the surface be as easy to love as Sanguines, but those parents who have made the effort to do so anyway have found it to be a rewarding experience.

The MelChlor child will not be as moody as the MelSan, but his Choleric determination will tend to make his bad moods last longer. He seems determined not to give up anything—not even a bad mood. This child usually does not get along well with other children, tends to be selfish, and does not like to share his toys, room, or personal effects. He often feels everyone is against him, and frequently retreats to the solitude of his own room to nurse his grudges. He can be hostile (even when he doesn't express it), and at three years old or even sooner he may oppose what you want him to do and the way you want it done. He may sulk long after punishment, blaming his parent in his mind rather than accepting his own faults. He criticizes himself, but does not like criticism from other people.

Even though the Choleric element is in a secondary position, its presence in this temperament blend may often give room for negative thinking. When the MelChlor gets older he will insist that his negativism is "just being realistic." In such a frame of mind he will usually make mountains out of molehills and refuse to take on a project or leadership role that is well within his capability.

The potential for success of these children can scarcely be overestimated. Watch carefully for the areas of their talents and then give special help to develop them. When they have done something well, give them plenty of approval to keep them going. Gradually their confidence will grow and they will develop rapidly in that field. After that, the thing to watch for is that they do not confine themselves to repeatedly do only the familiar and refuse to venture into other areas and to learn new things. One thing in his favor: the MelChlor is usually a good student.

The work habits of a MelChlor are never neat, even though he is a natural perfectionist. For this reason he needs to be encouraged at an early age to keep his room straight and put away his toys. Like the MelSan, he will probably have a critical spirit. This is the Melancholy side of him. If indulged, it will show in his face; conversely, if you teach him the art of thankful living (1 Thessalonians 5:18) he will develop a more cheerful countenance: "A joyful heart makes a cheerful face" (Proverbs 15:13a NASB).

Each new success in his young life will make it easier for him to experience other successes and unlock the door to his enormous potential. By looking at him through the rose-colored glasses of what he can become through God's grace, and by lovingly encouraging him to try things he automatically rejects as "too hard," you will help him build a self-image that will enable him to fit more comfortably into society and find a fulfilling service in the Lord's work.

MelPhleg

If you have a MelPhleg child, you may have a budding young genius on your hands. He won't be as hostile as the previous two Melancholic children and will either get along well with other children or will not play with them at all. He is inclined to be a loner, enjoying his own company. As he grows older he often gets excellent grades, and, if accepted lovingly by his parents for what he is, he can grow up to be a child of whom they are justifiably proud. But they must avoid trying to make him fit into another kind of mold. Usually he is quiet and subdued, so don't expect a Sanguine expressive reaction out of him.

All Melancholic children are sensitive, but this one most of all. He may be an emotional "clinger" when he is young. The best thing to do is pray for grace and let him cling. He needs your security and the assurance of your love. As he gets older he must receive a balance of that magic formula for child-raising: love, discipline, acceptance, and godly instruction. Don't let his "hurt" expressions keep you from punishing him for acts of rebellion, defiance, or sass. If your discipline is applied with love, he will probably get your message earlier than any other temperament. In spite of his sensitive nature, don't let him get by with selfishness when playing with other children. He is both self-centered and selfish, so he must learn to play and share with others. Don't be surprised if he is unusually self-conscious; in time he will grow out of most of it.

As the MelPhleg grows older, be consistent in teaching him social graces so he can learn to speak to adults as well as to his own peer group. He would rather "hermit" himself in his room when company comes over, but such a temptation should be discouraged until he has at least greeted the guests and spent a reasonable amount of time with them.

MelPhlegs often have a low threshold for embarrassment. One supersensitive 12-year-old MelPhleg daughter of a doctor friend of ours ran and hid in the bathroom when her mother first tried to instruct her in the use of wearing a bra. But gradually she came to accept her changing body and today is a lovely wife and mother. Although MelPhlegs need special help in developing the social areas of life, they usually are good students, cause little trouble, and have a responsive heart to spiritual instruction.

PhlegSan

The PhlegSan child is the most unabrasive of all temperaments. When a Phlegmatic has a 40 percent dose of Sanguine charm added, he can be a delightful child. Humanly speaking, these are usually the easiest of all people to get along with. As babies they are happy, contented cuddlers—"the perfect child."

They appear to be so perfect, in fact, that you may be blind to some of their weaknesses. All Phlegmatics have a motivational deficiency unless their parents have recognized that trait early and worked on it diligently. Neither the Phlegmatic nor the Sanguine is overly determined or self-controlled, so self-discipline in every area should be stressed. Don't permit him to leave his toys out overnight. Teach him early the need for keeping his room straight.

The PhlegSan child is easy to discipline and usually responds to rewards as well as he does to punishment. In fact, he often responds to a stern look as a form of punishment, because he has a strong desire to please. What rebellion he does possess could probably be handled by his third birthday—it just isn't that hard! Lovingly help him over his natural disease of "I can't"; that is, don't let him use "I can't" as a cop-out when you know he can, or else it will become a lifetime habit causing him to fall short of his full capabilities.

The PhlegSan child can be exasperating in school, for although he is capable enough, he never seems to put out to the level of his potential—it seems to take too much effort. He is a natural procrastinator and often fails to recall his assignment for the next day, or else his regular "forgetter" has caused him to leave his books at home.

In spite of his congenial ways, the PhlegSan can be stubborn, selfish, and stingy. If he doesn't have brothers and sisters in the home, he will have a hard time learning to share. A PhlegSan is timid and shy and needs to be drawn out of his shell. But an austere, critical, and loudly demanding parent will drive him deeper into his shell for protection, often inhibiting what social tendencies he might otherwise have. Parents of a PhlegSan will have better results if they remain calm and keep their voices at a moderate level. A parent can best help this child by teaching him to rely on the Lord, as shown through their own example, and build up his faith through a growing, personal relationship with Jesus Christ.

PhlegChlor

The PhlegChlor is not a great deal different from the PhlegSan except that he will be more disciplined and not as extroverted. The Choleric influence will make him goal-oriented and the most self-motivated of all the Phlegmatics, but he will never be a ball of fire.

That same influence, however, can also cause him to easily become angry; in fact, of all the Phlegmatics he will have the greatest problem with anger. Although he gets along well with others, as do most Phlegmatics, he is prone to be stubborn, selfish, and unyielding. This will usually reveal itself in his playing with other children. If he gets into a fight with one, it is usually when the Choleric influence in him is activated to protect his toys from being used by others. He tends to preserve them carefully. It is not uncommon for PhlegChlor ladies to have carefully stored their childhood dolls, or for men to have preserved their electric train collection.

It will take loving persistence on his parents' part to see that this little PhlegChlor is taught self-control in the form of finishing assignments and fulfilling obligations. The best time to start is between two and three years of age. Beware of TV: He can become an addict and live in a television dream world. When the real world around him becomes unpleasant, he will prefer the false world that television provides him.

This child's passive tendencies are compounded by a fear that often stifles his curiosity. He should be encouraged to cultivate his curiosity at a very early age. Although it may try your patience, let him crawl to his heart's content. It helps him later in life to be interested in many things. Parents will need to begin early to keep their PhlegChlor child motivated because he will have few motivation skills of his own. But he can be taught. As he becomes an achiever, his fear tendencies will be reduced to life size.

PhlegMel

The most introverted of all 12 temperament blends is the PhlegMel. PhlegMels are quieter than other children their age. Their crying is usually softer than others unless they are seriously hurt physically or emotionally. Like the other Phlegmatic children, they rarely defy you, though they may stubbornly drag their feet. No one can take more time to eat their dinner or to put their toys or clothes away, and it seems if you would let them, they would sleep or daydream all the time.

PhlegMels need to be encouraged to assert themselves more, to be given responsible time limits to get jobs done, and to be encouraged to attempt what is within their capabilities. If you don't prod him early in life, your PhlegMel will become a member of the "putterer society" and take forever to get anything done. Between his tendency to get everything organized before he starts something and his perfectionist traits, it usually takes him five times longer to do something than other children. School homework assignments or projects will rarely be done on time. If not cured in childhood, this trait will carry over into adulthood; it will make retaining employment difficult for the PhlegMel man or woman. Housework will be an endless chore and may often keep the family in turmoil.

As little tykes, PhlegMels are fearful and insecure and need lots of love to help them with self-acceptance. The child whose parents reject him will always have a difficult time accepting himself, but that is particularly true of anyone with a degree of Melancholic temperament. As a Christian parent, you have divine resources to assist your child with this problem. In fact, much of the Bible is written to help us overcome fear, worry, and anxiety. The PhlegMel child (like all others, actually) should be guided to memorize God's Word early and make his faith a vital part of his thinking. Read the story of Abraham in the Old Testament for a good example of a fear-dominated man who became a model of faith.

From Weakness to Strength

This brief description of the 12 blends in temperaments is not meant to be exhaustive. It is intended to help you see that every child has talents, strengths, and weaknesses, and should be considered in the light of his own individuality. Hopefully this concept will help you diagnose your child's primary and secondary temperaments and help you set goals that you wish to accomplish in the light of his needs.

You should develop a plan in advance designed to lovingly help your child strengthen his weaknesses. Many parents make the mistake of training all their children the same, and in so doing they often stifle latent creativity that should have been developed. Others have no plan for child-rearing, but expect to make up their mind on the spot as problems arise. We don't do that in building a house or taking a trip, so why should we be so haphazard about the important task of growing a child? As they say in business, "Plan your work and work your plan." Then you will truly enjoy your final product.

One Christian psychologist who is employed by a number of industrial corporations as a freelance consultant told us that his approach was to concentrate on a person's strengths and ignore his weaknesses. He studied people carefully for industry to make sure that they were temperamentally suited for the task they were assigned; then he encouraged them to concentrate on developing their strengths in the fulfillment of that task. His assumption was that their weaknesses would automatically take care of themselves.

We do not totally concur with this theory, but instead believe that in Galatians 5:22,23 the Holy Spirit provides every human being a strength for every conceivable weakness. These available spiritual resources should be used in the development of Christian children. However, that Christian psychologist's success in industry certainly underscores the fact that every good parent should find the area of his children's natural talents and strengths so he can help them cultivate a high degree of proficiency.

Your child will like himself better when you give him that help. If he likes himself more, you will find it easier for you to like him and for others to enjoy him as well. But the greatest result of encouraging him to develop his strengths and to overcome his weaknesses is that he will be more usable in the hand of God for whatever the perfect will of his heavenly Father might be for his life.

10

Night Feedings and Diapers

Every time a baby is born significant changes must be made by the family, but the first baby seems to require the most adjustments by the mother. The reality of her new role in life doesn't hit her until she comes home from the hospital and finds herself face-to-face with a brand-new, breathing baby who is depending on his mother for everything.

I was certainly not adequately prepared for the days that followed, and I think many other mothers are not ready for the drastic change that follows the birth of a child. This new life has come to stay 24 hours a day and won't go away!

Most new mothers are nervous when they realize that they now bear full responsibility for the life of this tiny human being. A new mother may feel so inadequate and unsure of herself that she worries about every little thing. If the baby is sleeping, she checks often to see if he is breathing. If he cries, she is concerned that he is ill. Such insecurity may cause her frequent tension, but she would rather die than admit these feelings to anybody else. If only she knew that most new mothers feel the same way! She thinks that every other mother has a natural "mother instinct" and that she alone is not prepared for this new role.

In addition to the new mother's feelings of inadequacy, there is another set of feelings which she tries to stifle, but they remain just under the surface—feelings of resentment. This resentment can result from feeling tied down, no longer free to go and come as she did formerly. Her time is no longer her own, for now she has a little creature that demands a lot of care and attention. Her feelings of resentment are entirely normal, but unfortunately nobody can prepare her for this aspect of her new experience.

Another reason a mother may resent her new baby is that she assumes her child will automatically bring her and her husband closer together, but often quite the opposite happens. Instead of bringing them together, the innocent new baby may act as a wedge which separates them. The husband is often jealous of the attention given to the new baby. His wife's time used to belong to him, but now he may think that 100 percent of the responsibility is hers and that he is shoved out in the cold.

There is a growing trend, however, and a good one, for the fathers to take more care of the new baby and to thereby develop a loving bond with this child. The Christian young couple must accept these emotions as part of the normal adjustment period for both the husband and wife. They are only temporary. Each mother will need to find her own ideas and methods of making this threesome a close unit. It will help her to remember that these feelings of inadequacy, resentment, and panic are all very normal, and as she gains experience, her confidence will grow.

An Original Created by God

Let me remind you of the uniqueness of your baby. There is no one else in the world like your child. That baby is literally one of a kind. He is his own temperament. His label can read "An original created by God." So if your baby's development doesn't match the time schedule of the "typical" baby found in many books, don't jump to the conclusion that there is something wrong with him. Don't try to force him into some mental picture you have read in a book of what the "average" baby ought to be like. Let him be unique!

Your role as a parent is of extreme importance in helping your child develop this uniqueness. He must have your help and encouragement. If you can accept his individual patterns of eating and sleeping, as well as his babyish temperament and moods, it will be easier for you to accept his individuality at later stages of development. You will be a happier parent if you give up trying to make your child fit into your pattern and design. Give him the freedom to develop naturally according to his own temperament.

Stages of Development

Each child goes through the same general stages of development and in the same order, but on a different time schedule. The most important stages in development will be during the first few years of his life. You are programming him for a high level of intellectual attainment. This period in his life moves in a furious pace, never to be equaled again in a similar period. About half of the intellectual capacity of an adult has been developed by the age of four and 80 percent by the age of eight (this is intelligence, not information). That is why it is so important for the child to be in the loving care of his parents during these first important years. After that, with schooling and environment, his mental abilities can be altered only about 20 percent.

The next section of this book has more to do with your beginning experiences with your new baby than it does with his temperament. But keep in mind that if you give him a good start from the earliest days of his life, it will be easier to help mold his temperament in later years. The following four stages during the development of your young child are only approximate time schedules. Remember, your child is unique—one of a kind.

First Three Months

Your child's learning begins at the moment of his birth. He is never too young to be learning something. He very quickly acquires his basic outlook on life and develops either a basic sense of trust and security or one of emotional insecurity and distrust. The environment you provide for him will play a large role in determining what his self-concept will be.

There are seven basic needs that an infant has during this period of development. The fulfillment of these needs will be the beginning of his sense of security and self-image.

1. *Hunger.* Infants seem to be all mouth and stomach, but a baby also feels intense hunger pangs. After he has been fed, he will go back to sleep until the hunger pangs wake him up again. As he grows older he will have longer periods of wakefulness. His hunger can be easily satisfied by simply feeding him. The great controversy is whether it should be breast-feeding or bottle-feeding. Isn't it a shame that we have complicated something that was designed to be so simple? God designed a mother's breast to produce milk only after giving birth to a baby.

The benefit of breast-feeding is that it automatically involves cuddling and stroking, which are necessary ingredients in the development of each child. Breast-feeding is strongly recommended by most medical care workers. Unfortunately, the bottle-fed baby often has his bottle propped up when mother gets too busy to sit down and hold him. I recommend breast-feeding very strongly, but you have the freedom to choose the method you will use. If you choose bottle-feeding, be sure you can discipline yourself to hold and cuddle your baby for every feeding, or you will be depriving him of an important ingredient for proper development.

Now the question comes up: When to feed your baby? Should he be fed on a rigid time schedule or simply when he gets hungry? Remember that he is an original creation and that a time schedule which suits one baby may not be satisfying to another. Each baby's hunger may vary from day to day. When he is hungry he becomes frustrated. He wants to be fed "now." One medical doctor says that when a baby has to wait a half-hour for his feeding, it is as if an adult had to wait three days.

When the infant is hungry and is not fed, he reacts by crying. The longer he waits, the louder and more insistent his crying becomes. As more time passes, the crying changes in quality and tone. Now his crying takes on a tone of anger. He is furious because no one is paying any attention to him.

Finally he begins to learn that no amount of crying will bring attention to his needs. He may react with continued anger or he may become listless and apathetic, weakened and resigned that no one will respond. Some of this response can be attributed to the temperament he is becoming. Whatever he does, he has learned a beginning distrust of life and those around him.

How much better it would be for the child if you would respect his individuality from birth. You can help build the foundation for a strong and healthy self-concept if you feed him when he shows hunger.

2. *Warmth.* This is one area that most parents do not need to be reminded about. In fact, many pediatricians claim that some young mothers overdress infants so they are kept too warm. The important thing to remember is that babies should not be allowed to get chilled. A dry diaper against his body is much more warming than a wet one. Wind is one chill factor to which small babies should not be exposed.

3. *Sleep.* The baby will take care of this need himself if the first two needs have been cared for. When he has had enough sleep, he will wake up. It is a good habit not to keep the house hushed for the baby to sleep. Keep the noise in the house at a reasonable, normal volume and the baby will develop the ability to sleep in these surroundings.

Occasionally a baby may wake up crying during the middle of the night for some unknown reason. He may have stomach distress or colic, and you will feel helpless to ease his discomfort. Your stroking or cuddling may not comfort him or stop the crying. Moments like these can be very trying on young parents. In the wee hours of the morning you may feel frustrated, panicky, or even angry that your sleep has been disturbed and that you can do nothing for the child.

If your feelings get out of control and you find yourself handling the baby roughly, leave the room immediately and get alone to ask God to give you more patience and to calm your emotions. If your anger repeats itself and you cannot control your feelings at a time like this, then seek the aid of a minister who can help and advise you before you bring bodily harm to a helpless, innocent child.

4. *Physical Cuddling and Stroking.* Unless your baby experiences being rocked, cuddled, stroked, talked to, and sung to, he cannot know he is loved. It must be demonstrated in a physical way. As you rock your infant, the soft tone of your voice as you gently sing to him, or the comforting tones of the father's lower voice, will help him to know he is loved. Love him all you want! Loving never "spoiled" any baby.

5. *Bodily Exercise.* There is a limit to what your little fellow can do in the way of bodily exercise. However, there should be a certain period during the day when he is allowed to swing his arms and legs freely without being swaddled with blankets. While traveling through South America I observed many different tribes of Indians who dressed their infants in swaddling clothes with arms and legs wrapped snugly in a down-stretched position. There was no room for movement of any kind. Even up to the age of two or more the infants are most often strapped on the mother's back with little or no leg exercise at all. Just

as you must gradually develop your children's minds intellectually, so their physical bodies need this day-by-day development of their limbs through exercise.

6. *Diaper Attention.* Attend to the changing of diapers with a matter-of-fact attitude. The parent who communicates dislike and disapproval toward the messy diaper may succeed in making the job of toilet training more difficult later on. You will later benefit by taking a more relaxed attitude toward diaper changing. As long as the infant is not in a cold room, he will probably not be bothered by a wet or messy diaper. This doesn't mean you should neglect him so that he develops a bad case of diaper rash, but it does mean that there is no need to awaken him just to change a diaper that may seem unpleasant to you.

7. *Sensory and Intellectual Stimulation.* Each child inherits a certain maximum intelligence potential which he might reach as he grows up. However, whether or not he reaches his maximum intelligence will depend a great deal on how much sensory and intellectual stimulation he receives during the first few years of his life. He needs to be able to handle objects that he can smell, hear, put in his mouth, and even suck. But take care that he doesn't have access to objects which are small enough for him to choke on.

Three to Six Months

This period is a time of transition from infancy to babyhood. He begins to investigate his world by reaching out to things. He explores his environment with his eyes, ears, and mouth. At this age everything starts to go into his mouth to be tested. This is his method of discovering things around him. His hands are used to grasp and feel objects and then to explore them further by trying them in his mouth. Don't be alarmed if he begins to suck his fingers. This is a built-in pacifier that God has given him to keep him quiet so he can learn about the sights and sounds of his new world. The fetus has already achieved hand-to-mouth contact before birth, so look on it as a normal step in this stage of development.

Rattles and rubber squeeze toys are good at this stage. Examine them carefully to be sure there are no detachable parts that your baby could swallow. A contrasting texture for him would be soft, cuddly toys.

This is about the only period when a child can be confined to a playpen. He is too young to move himself about, but he enjoys being around other people. After this stage he wants the freedom of maneuvering himself from place to place, and I would recommend putting the playpen in storage.

Six to Nine Months

Give your baby time to adjust to a new situation. Proceed slowly when you are showing him a new person. If the introduction results in crying, he is telling you he is afraid. It is quite common at this stage for infants to develop an anxiety toward strangers.

During this period his babbling and vocalizing will increase. He will probably expose his first tooth and may even become an active member of the family by crawling. He has learned a form of communication of his very own.

Through grunts and gestures he can usually indicate what he wants.

Water play is probably the most soothing and relaxing activity for a baby at this age. He enjoys splashing but is still unsteady, so the water must be kept shallow to prevent him from having a fearful experience or even drowning. Do not leave him unattended. By this age your baby should not be kept in the playpen but should be allowed a corner of a room where there is nothing that could endanger him. He can often play happily by himself for a half-hour at a time. He enjoys playing with simple household objects such as Tupperware-type containers.

Nine to Twelve Months

At this stage your baby may already be walking, or just about to start in a few more months. He will no longer be passive and quiet while you are changing a diaper or dressing him, unless he is a high percentage of Phlegmatic. The Sanguine will make a game of it to see if you can diaper a fast-moving object. He will begin to show unsophisticated coordination with games such as patty-cake. Your baby will be able to understand a great many things that are said to him. You can teach him by speaking to him in single words when you are identifying objects.

This is the time to introduce books to your child. He will probably put them in his mouth, but remember that this is the way he explores almost all new objects. His books should be made of cloth or heavy cardboard and should be filled with simple pictures and single words. Let him taste or pat or stroke the pages. Your proper response to this will lay the foundation for his love and appreciation for good books.

11

Toddlers and Toilet Training

The toddler stage begins as soon as your baby learns to walk. This is a great day for him because now he can explore certain areas of the house that he could not reach before. Even when he was crawling, he was rather limited as to where he could go or how fast he could get there, but now new worlds and closets are open to him to explore.

Childproofing Your House

While your child is learning to explore new things, you will be busy learning how to childproof the house for his protection. At this point a mother has to decide which she wants— a spotless house and a toddler who is passive and full of self-doubts, or a somewhat littered house and a toddler who has a good self-image and developing self-confidence.

Too often toddlers are raised in a house designed for adults, and their curiosity and desire to explore is held back with restraint. The curiosity that the toddler shows at this stage is the same curiosity which will make him successful in school and his occupation in later life. Curiosity is an aid to learning. He needs to be guarded so as not to bring harm to himself, but do not restrain his desire for wanting to learn. Remove the dangerous and breakable objects from his reach. The experts tell us that safety precautions to childproof your house could prevent 50 to 90 percent of the accidents which seriously injure or kill babies and toddlers.

Protected But Not Overprotected

This faster-moving baby needs to be protected but not overprotected. There is a vast difference. He needs parents to protect him against dangers he is too naive to guard against. But if a situation holds no danger and you are being overprotective, this could fill your child with fear and possibly affect his ability to cope with normal situations as he develops. Abnormal fears can be instilled in your child's emotions by the way you protect him and react to normal situations in life.

Finger-Sucking

If your child has been a finger-sucker during his first year, you can expect that it will taper off slightly in his second year. He will be more active in using his fingers and will be able to entertain himself with a greater variety of things. When he or she becomes tired, unhappy, or bored, you can expect his fingers to go back into his mouth again.

I encourage mothers to introduce a blanket or stuffed animal to their child and hope that it will become a replacement for finger-sucking. There is no shame in seeing a young child able to invest some of his ability to love and care for a doll, a teddy bear, or even a worn-out soft blanket. He should be able to count on this source of comfort when he needs it, and for as long as he needs it.

Don't be concerned that your little "Linus" will grow up to take his blanket to college. If your attitude toward his blanket has been normal and not disapproving, then he will make the adjustment in due time. As children mature they seem to be able to satisfy these needs with relationships to other people and to involve themselves in things that are more interesting.

Eating Habits

Even at this young age many parents allow their children to develop atrocious eating habits. I have walked through a grocery store on many occasions and watched while mothers with small children in their carts have loaded their baskets with sugars, starches, and prepared foods that have little or no food value. Excess sugars and starches will contribute to the decay of children's teeth and sometimes even to diabetes. Not only are these foods harmful in themselves, but they also satisfy young appetites and keep children from eating foods that are more nutritious.

Parents of babies and young children have the opportunity to start their children off with good eating habits right from the start. Make the diet balanced and the rule so definite that the children accept them as a matter of course, particularly in these early years when their bodies are developing and need the benefits of good dietary habits.

There can be rare exceptions for treats, but these should be held to a minimum. Youngsters often become choosy and finicky about their food at this age and may eat less. This is probably a blessing because if they continued eating at the same rate as in the first year of life, they would become as wide as they are tall.

Your child's appetite will vary from day to day, just as yours will. Mother, don't fret or feel worried that your child is not eating enough! All too often mothers worry about little Betsy not eating her vegetables. The more she pressures little Betsy to eat vegetables, the more Betsy balks. The less the child eats, the more worried and anxious mother becomes, until finally the mother has a full-fledged eating problem on her hands where before no problem existed.

This is completely unnecessary. Remember, a mother has on her side the natural hunger of the child. Offer Betsy a well-balanced diet and leave her alone. Sooner or later her hunger pangs will take over and she will eat what you offer her. Be sure you are not offering snacks of sweets and starches, however. Give her the freedom to turn against certain foods. When you don't make an issue of the matter, she may decide next week that it is her very favorite. I remember the pediatrician for one of my children telling me that he had never known a child to die of starvation when there was food set before him!

At some time during this stage of development, your child will decide that he wants to spoon-feed himself.

There is only one way for him to learn and that is to take the spoon and begin. Have a good supply of wipes nearby! It takes a lot of drips and spills to accomplish spoon-feeding, but it is a great step toward independence.

Toilet Training

Most American mothers are in a great hurry to get rid of the diaper routine; it is a nuisance to always take spare diapers everywhere you go, not to mention the mess and the odor. But even though it is a great day when a child has graduated from diapers and can take care of his own detail, trying to toilet train him too early can be a psychological disaster, or at least a waste of the mother's time and efforts.

One noted medical doctor has said that a child does not have the neuromuscular maturation he needs to control his bladder and bowels until after two years of age. He even went so far as to say that whenever he finds a youngster over the age of five who is a bed-wetter, it is very possible that the attempt to toilet train the child was rushed; the child was simply not ready.

Another well-respected child psychologist states that a child is not ready for bowel control before his second year or for urinary control before his third year. He adds that a child should not be considered a bed-wetter until five years of age. So be patient, dear mother, and remind yourself with every diaper you change that you are helping your child to develop a normal childhood that will lead to an adjusted adulthood.

Educating with Toys

Books are a very important part of your child's life at this stage. He will still need books that are made of cloth or heavy cardboard because he will undoubtedly investigate them by tearing or chewing on them. You can begin reading simple nursery rhymes or Bible story books geared to the toddler's age level. He will soon be able to identify single words from a story that is repeated over and over, such as "Jesus" when he sees a baby in a manger.

Numerous playthings are available to help develop his large and small muscles. A few examples are a low slide, a small jungle gym, a sandbox with pail and shovel, a pail of water for making mud pies, cuddly animals, dolls, and music that deals with sounds and rhythm.

Spanking

Spanking a two-year-old is necessary only when you must repeatedly protect him from danger. Be careful not to falsely interpret the behavior of the toddler as being hostile or destructive. It may be that he is just exercising his curiosity and behaving normally for his age. A two-year-old child may be unable to understand adult reasoning when he reaches out to play with an electric wall plug. He is too young to be allowed to suffer natural consequences, so a hand spanking is obviously necessary in this case. His derriere will be well-padded with diapers, so a sting on the hands as he reaches out to touch the wall plug will remind him that this was an unpleasant experience without giving him bodily harm.

The first signs of temperament traits may begin to reveal themselves during this stage. The wise parent will be alert and able to deal with the demonstration of the child's weaknesses.

The Choleric toddler will show signs of being a bully to other children, will be very selfish with his toys, and will definitely begin to show a strong self-will. This young child needs to have his will directed toward good. When his strong will persists there will be a point in time to break his will but not his spirit. Too many parents excuse their child's behavior by saying that Cindy would be different if she just had a brother or sister, whereas in reality that would probably make little difference, since she may simply be acting like a Choleric. Her great need is to have parents who are willing to deal with that selfishness and to discipline her with strong, consistent training. After three years of age that strong will becomes harder to break with each passing year.

The Sanguine toddler will have a hot temper and may reveal it by screaming and turning bright red in the face as his body stiffens. His anger can flare up so fast that before the watchful eye of the parent he can pick up a toy and fling it at the one who angered him. A moment later he can turn on the charm and act like a different person. In spite of his copious tears of remorse, this uncontrollable anger needs to be dealt with as soon as it is displayed and before he becomes dangerous. He cannot be permitted to harm other children with his fits of rage.

The Phlegmatic toddler will remain rather passive at this age and will be more of an observer than a participant. Do not ignore this child just because he does not demand attention. His weaknesses will take a bit longer before they begin to show and will probably make him an easier child to deal with at this stage.

The Melancholic toddler can be recognized by his whining disposition. He is also inclined to be more of a clinger when left at Grandma's or with a babysitter. This child needs to be loved and given a sense of security more than the others. Make sure that punishments are given only for direct acts of rebellion and are followed with love and tenderness that assure the child of your forgiveness. The parent needs to be very sensitive to what best helps the child and what is really behind the whining and cling- ing—gaining his own way or a real sense of insecurity.

Alternating Years

The experts tell us that between birth and five years of age children are difficult to raise and cope with on alternating years. In other words, the odd years (one-three-five) seem to be the years when a child is generally a pleasure to have around, while the even years (two-four) are the trying years when the child is in a transition stage and acts more like a tearful and destructive monster than an adorable child. Probably most parents would agree that the age of 2½ years is the most exasperating time of a child's preschool training. Remember, just about the time you feel you can't live with this little unreasonable child any longer, he will turn three and begin to change for the better.

12

Trusty Threes

You can expect a new spirit of cooperation from your three-year-old. Prior to this time one might think that the child instead of the parents was running the family. But if you have responded properly to his demands of control, you should now begin to have a more enjoyable home environment.

The three-year-old seems to have a greater desire to cooperate and win the approval of his older sisters and brothers, and also his parents, than when he was two. He is able to work more patiently at dressing himself or at similar tasks instead of exploding, as he may have done previously. He has a greater ability to interact with other children in sharing and taking turns.

This should be a delightful time for both parents and child because he is more content. He loves his parents, he enjoys life, and he is generally at peace with the world. However, I would not want to deceive you into thinking your troubles are over. They may be lessened, but there are still challenges ahead as your child moves toward maturity.

At the age of three he begins to crave playmates for companionship. For certain temperaments the desire for independence will cause him to want to have limited separations from his mother. Moms should not feel threatened when this occurs because this is a normal part of his development. He still wants the security and protection of his mother but needs some independence and companionship with his peers.

This is an important step for your child and needs to be handled very matter-of-factly. He needs to learn how to cope with short periods of separation in order to build toward longer periods when school begins. He should be encouraged to venture out to play with the neighborhood children and attend Sunday school for his age group. If there is a good nursery school near you, I suggest letting him attend for three or four hours a week to start. Notice that I am suggesting *limited* periods of separation. I do not recommend that children be enrolled in a full-time nursery school at this young age. Too much of their development is based on the mother-child relationship, even at three years.

Swinging Back and Forth

As the child enters his third year he will swing back and forth from the extreme independence of "I can do it myself" to the limp and helpless "I can't do it," so that his mother must do it for him. It is wise for parents to have consistent rules and limits at this stage, but not to make too many demands for absolute conformity. However, the child must learn to conform to what his parents and society expect of him and at the same time develop a healthy self-identity. You must weigh the limits and demands carefully. They should be reasonable and consistent and you should be able to justify these limits to yourself and to your child.

At this young age you need not be rigid about what is "feminine" or "masculine." There is no harm in allowing a three-year-old girl to play with trucks and fire engines if that is what she wants, and there is no harm in a three-year-old boy playing house with dolls if he chooses. Many mothers provide old dress-up clothes for the girls to engage in imaginary dramatic play, but what about the boys? Usually if they want to play they must wear the dresses, hats, and high-heeled shoes. If you provide some of Father's old jeans, hats, and boots, then he can enter the dramatic performance as a man.

However, don't be alarmed if he should choose to wear the dress one day, because the next day he will probably prefer the jeans and boots. Such choices do not indicate that he will be abnormal. The important factor is Mother and Father's attitude toward the little girl or boy. If Mom and Dad encourage the daughter's femininity with her docile, sweet spirit and ruffle her curls, then the son deserves equal attention in his nature of boyish toughness and mischievousness.

The most important person in a young child's life is his mother, so both boys and girls tend to identify with her from the very beginning. They spent nine months bonding with her in the womb, and after birth (under normal conditions) they have spent the major portion of each day of their young life with her. Little boys and little girls love their mother and want to be like her.

However, most boys and girls begin to branch off into their own separate psychological development after a short time. It is very important for fathers to spend time with their preschool sons to compensate for this lack of male influence (preschool daughters need the male relationship also). Dads, this early contact with your children will build good father-and-son or father-and-daughter relationships for later years. Both little girls and little boys need models to imitate. Simple projects could be planned with Dad and the child.

How Much Control?

The parent who is Melancholic and Choleric tends to be more rigid and domineering than the other temperaments. His demands can be far too numerous, and it results in overcontrolling his children. The mother with the newly waxed kitchen floor or the freshly hung bathroom towels needs to remember that the house should be designed for the children, not the children for the house. Parental overcontrol is not very tolerant of childish impulses and emotional outbursts typical of children this age. Their responses will vary, depending greatly on the temperament of each child.

1. *The Sanguine child.* Overcontrol will be bitterly resisted by the Sanguine, and through his tears he will spout off loudly because of the unreasonable restrictions put on him. This whole stage of development becomes a

battleground of wills between parent and child, and regardless of who wins the battle, the child loses the potential of developing his individuality at this stage. This may well be the beginning of producing a rebellious child.

2. *The Choleric child.* The Choleric child may be able to control his outward feelings more than the Sanguine, but inwardly he will resist it just as bitterly and will hold out to the bitter end rather than give in. Unfortunately, he will become frustrated and eventually rebellious because he is not able to develop his own individuality and be himself.

3. *The Phlegmatic child.* This temperament may respond without any unpleasant confrontations. However, the final result could well be a quiet, passive, fearful child who could easily become a timid, unaggressive adult afraid to venture out and try new things. Since this temperament tends to be fearful anyway, he needs encouragement to be more assertive rather than to be held down.

4. *The Melancholic child.* This child may appear to conform to the parental overcontrol, but inwardly he will seethe with hostility. He will grudgingly do what is expected of him, but will become sneaky and do his own thing. His hostility may be shown in destroying something valuable or pinching baby brother. The Melancholic may grow up to be a narrow-minded, self-righteous person, outwardly full of pious, moral rules but inwardly full of hostility.

Equally harmful to a three-year-old is the problem of too little control from the parents. The Sanguine and Phlegmatic parents will be most guilty of this—the Phlegmatics because they are loving and do not like confrontations, and the Sanguines because they are happy-go-lucky and inconsistent, and have an everything-is-going-to-work-out-okay attitude. When their children refuse to abide by the parental limits and controls, they immediately relax the limits and let their children have their own way. Soon the children play the role of parent and take over the control of the house.

These children are going to have a difficult time when they enter school and find that the teacher and the children require a reasonable amount of conformity to the rules. Parents can greatly aid their children's adjustment to school and society by helping them learn to conform to rules at home.

Toilet Training

This section is not designed to give you specific instructions on how to toilet train your child. Numerous books by medical doctors go into great detail on this subject. I would simply like to consider the effects of improper toilet training, as well as your attitude toward teaching this new skill.

You cannot toilet train your child unless he is willing to be trained. The old adage "You can lead a horse to water but you can't make him drink" can be related to toilet training also: "You can lead a child to the toilet but you can't make him go." The motivating power that causes him to give up his old convenient method of elimination is his good relationship with his mother. He enjoys being rewarded by her love and attention when he succeeds in this new way of life. Successful toilet training requires a good relationship between mother and child.

If you put pressure on him to learn too fast and you have not slowly paved the way, then he could easily feel helpless and frustrated. This is a complex undertaking for a child. Punishment for failures or accidents can produce fear, anger, stubbornness, and even defiance in the child. Punishment should never be used in toilet training.

A few simple suggestions for mothers regarding toilet training are to approach it in a casual and relaxed manner. Be matter of-fact and do not be in a hurry. Even though every kid in the block was toilet trained when he was the age of your child, you must remember that your son or daughter is unique. He is an individual. He will make a lot of mistakes, but we all do when we are learning a new skill.

Bedtime Ritual

Children at this age love rituals, so to make bedtime a more enjoyable experience, it is a good idea to establish a "bedtime ritual." This can be a very beneficial time when the father shares in preparing the child for bed each night. Unfortunately, this is not a very good time for rough play, since this overstimulates the child and makes it hard for him to go to sleep and may even produce restlessness during the night.

The ideal schedule would be to have active play as soon as the father gets home from work in the afternoon and before dinner. This could be anything from rolling or catching a ball to wrestling on the floor. If you cannot work out this ideal schedule, and since rough play is of great value between father and child, you may have to work it in after dinner. A brief period could be designated for active play (maybe ten minutes). Then proceed to the tub for a bath.

Most children look at bathtime simply as playing, and Dad could take advantage of this fact by supervising the bath with boats and floating toys. After the pajamas are on is an ideal time for book-reading or storytelling. Dad may desire to enter the picture at this point and perform the nightly ritual of telling or reading a story, or even making up a story if he is so inclined. (Children love made-up stories with funny noises.) The last story should be a comforting Bible story such as Jesus loving the little children, the shepherd finding the little lost lamb, or Jesus as a baby in the manger. There are numerous stories to pick from.

Then let your child pray. Children love to talk to Jesus in their own simple, floundering way. They have great faith and expectations, so build on it. A goodnight kiss and a hug will finish it off for the night. All this ritual can take from 30 to 40 minutes, depending on what you include.

One father complained when I told him that the bedtime ritual could take about 30 minutes and I suggested that he do it with his child. He felt he didn't have that much time to give, yet the same dad could find time later in the evening to sit for several hours and watch the NBA playoffs on television. There are only a few years when you can tuck them into bed and give them that goodnight kiss. A few years later many a parent wishes he had been more consistent and willing when he had the opportunity.

Bedtime should be a time of pleasure for the child; you want him to look forward to this fun experience. You do not want him to dread or fear it, though some children may do so because they are afraid of the dark. Don't send your child to a dark room if he is afraid. If a soft light in his room will eliminate this fear, then by all means let him have the light. You need not worry that he will grow up always needing a light in his room. As he grows older he will overcome many of these childish fears if you have been understanding and considerate of him at this age.

Questions and Answers

One of the greatest gifts you can give your child is to share with him your knowledge of the world as you answer his questions. The ideal response would be that you answer all the questions your child asks, even if the answer is that you do not know the answer. No parent is able to answer every question asked at this age, so don't feel guilty if occasionally you suggest that he play quietly so you can have time to think.

If parents realized the value of these questions and their answers, they would have a better attitude toward them. Always try to keep an open communication between parent and child. This interchange between parent and child teaches some of the most important courses on everyday living that he will ever experience.

Many parents live very busy lives. When they are too busy to listen to their children, then they are simply too busy. The parents who want to be successful in child-raising will have to discipline themselves to listen. When they do, they are assuring the child that they really care about him and that they think he is important. This is the way to build a good self-image in your child. You will also learn what is going on in his mind if you listen carefully to what he has to say. Being alert to his talk may give you sufficient warning when fears or insecurities begin to build up in his thoughts. The day may come when you would give anything to have him talk to you.

The parents of a Sanguine child will have to do more listening because the Sanguine does more talking. The Phlegmatic child is not too talkative, so his parents will have to be sensitive regarding what he doesn't talk about. It is wise parents who encourage him to talk and to express himself, and they can best accomplish this by listening to him attentively.

First Image of Heavenly Father

A little child relates unknown things to what he knows. He first hears about the heavenly Father but cannot see Him, so he relates this unknown Father to his earthly father whom he knows. This is not restricted to just the age of three. It is mentioned here because this is where it usually begins, but it will carry on for the next few years. He learns of God's love by watching his parents. He learns of God's mercy and forgiveness by watching his parents. Be sure you are giving him an honest picture of what he can expect from his own heavenly Father.

Books

Books for this age should be well-constructed. Just because they go in his mouth, do not be deceived into thinking that your child is too young to profit from books. One of the earliest ways to stimulate him intellectually is by reading to him and acquainting him with the great wealth of knowledge that comes from books.

A child in this stage is fascinated by words and word play. He loves nursery rhymes with their rhythm and repetition of sounds. He likes familiar nursery tales such as "Chicken Little" or "The Three Little Pigs." He will be able to recognize what is coming next in the story and will say it with you as you read to him.

He enjoys looking at the book and touching it. Ask him questions about the story or ask him to find things in the illustrations. He will love it. Most often he will have a favorite book that he will want you to read to him every day. If you change one phrase he will probably object and correct you.

A few good books are:

The Cat in the Hat Beginner Book Dictionary, by Dr. Seuss (Random House).

The Giant Nursery Book of Things That Go, by George Zaffo (Doubleday).

Goodnight, Moon, by Margaret Wise Brown (Harper & Row).

Tall Book of Nursery Tales, illustrated by Feodor Rojankovsky (Harper & Row).

The Tale of Peter Rabbit, by Beatrix Potter (Warne).

Millions of Cats, by Wanda Gag (Coward-McCann).

Series of Pattibooks, by Mary E. LeBar (Scripture Press).

Many other good books can be purchased at your local Christian bookstore. Go in and browse around.

This list is very scanty, but it is only intended to whet your appetite to research the vast number of books available for your toddler. It is inaccurate to place books in strict age categories because maturity and understanding vary so much. Parents, examine every book carefully before bringing it home to read to your child. You alone can determine what will best suit him.

The reading experience can be a pleasure to both reader and listener when you have a warm little body sitting snugly beside you and together you go off to the adventure that a good book provides. It is an experience to remember.

13

Frisky Fours

Suddenly the three-year-old who has made great strides and has been well-coordinated may now begin to demonstrate almost a reversal in his coordination. He may appear to be clumsy and awkward at times. New habits may begin, such as picking his nose, biting his nails, or sucking his thumb.

He loves to play with other children his age, even though at times he may not get along with them too well. His relationships may be stormy and violent, filled with demands, shoving, and hitting. There is often a good deal of bossiness and belligerence in the four-year-old, and his emotional extremes may vary from shyness one moment to boisterousness the next.

He has also learned that there is a whole group of words that his parents do not approve of, and he can usually get attention when using them. This seems to be a period of testing authority because he loves to defy orders or requests. Because of this, four-year-olds need firmness.

Their scrapping can best be dealt with by social isolation. The parent should matter-of-factly say something like, "You and Chris aren't playing very well this morning so you will need to play by yourself now. You will be able to play together when I think you can play peaceably again." This will be a motivating factor for him to shape up so he can return to his friends.

I agree with a noted child psychologist when he stated that a four-year-old reminded him of the man described by Stephen Leacock, who jumped on his horse and rode off rapidly in all directions. The four-year-old does not know where he is going even though he is filled with activity. He can be a confused blend of silly and serious, quiet and noisy, cheerful and whiny, indifferent and cooperative, agreeable and disagreeable, shy and aggressive.

Developing Physically and Intellectually

Because of the great need for the biological development of Mr. Frisky Four, he has an intense drive to release his energy. He needs to climb, wiggle, run, jump, and yell to accomplish this. Therefore he needs to have constructive outlets for his energy, or else he will find destructive ones. Parents have difficulty accepting this fact, especially if they enjoy peace and quiet. If you give your child ample opportunity to run, jump, climb, or crawl, you will be aiding his intellectual skills when he starts school. (For a more thorough study on this you might consult the book by Radler and Kephart entitled *Success Through Play*.)

Temper Tantrums

All children are capable of having a temper tantrum, regardless of their temperament. However, the Sanguine will be the most likely to scream at the top of his lungs and throw himself on the floor in a fit of rage. The Choleric also has this potential if he has had little discipline. But the Melancholic can muster up a good tantrum if he feels like he has been dealt with unjustly. The most unlikely tantrum-thrower is the Phlegmatic, since he is rather passive and peace-loving. But any child who becomes so enraged that all he can do is cry, scream, or throw himself on the floor will occasionally have a temper tantrum.

If you give in to his demands during a tantrum, you will reinforce it and encourage him to throw another tantrum the next time he wants his way. This outburst of emotion results from the struggle for power within him. When he emerges victorious in such a struggle, the child has learned that he can gain control by throwing tantrums.

Contrary to what many others have said, I firmly believe the most effective method of handling a tantrum is to respond to his anger. A parent should, first of all, be sure to have control of his own emotions and ask the Holy Spirit to guard and guide him through this experience. In other words, be careful not to respond in rage or frustration. Then firmly send the child to his room until he has calmed down and gained control of himself.

When the temper fit has ended, then the parent can better communicate with the child and point out his uncalled-for behavior and respond with a sound spanking or an appropriate action that teaches his child. A spanking given in the midst of the tantrum will often result in a further struggle for power. Do not allow yourself to be brought into that struggle. The great temptation is to raise your voice and scream at your child for his behavior. When you respond in that way, you have lost—you have lost the struggle and you have lost control of the situation.

Beginning Sex Education

The age at which children begin to ask questions will vary a great deal. Some observant children will notice very early that girls sit and boys stand when they go to the bathroom, or that boys have an extra body part that girls don't have. However, there will be some who will be oblivious to the difference at this age. One little boy was looking at a very small nude infant waiting for his bath. His mother, also watching, asked her son if the baby was a girl or a boy. He quickly responded, "I can't tell when his clothes are off."

The important thing to remember about this subject is to face questions with a calm, matter-of-fact attitude. This will be the greatest contribution you can make to your child's sexual development. Answer each question as it comes and answer it honestly. When your four-year-old daughter discovers that her brother has a penis, matter-of-factly call it a penis, just as you would identify his knee or toe.

Some little girls may feel that they have been short-changed by not having a penis. Occasionally a little boy may become fearful that his may get cut off like his sister's was. A mother's healthy attitude toward these fears in children can help to make them short-lived. I appreciated what one medical doctor suggested as an answer to both boys and girls to help them accept with confidence their bodies as they are. Simply explain to your boy or girl that fathers and boys have a penis and mothers and girls have a special bag built inside their tummy called a uterus. This bag is a special place where God makes babies grow. This should satisfy their questions for the time being; but, believe me, more questions will come later.

Effects of TV-Watching

Statistics prepared by the A.C. Neilsen Company, the television rating and research firm, show that boys and girls between the ages of two and five watch an average of 23 1/4 hours or more of television a week, with the figure going down in the summer and up in the winter. Furthermore, children who remain "typical" viewers from the age of 3 through 17 will end up spending more time in front of the television set than in school.

Many experiments have been conducted across the country to determine the effect of TV on children who watch it from 20 to 25 hours a week. On the positive side are the suggestions that TV broadens a child's vocabulary and increases his awareness of the world around him. However, the electronic babysitter results in young children watching far too much television and certainly some wrong programs.

Dr. William Glasser, educator, psychiatrist, and director of the Los Angeles center for training teachers in reality therapy, advocates that TV limits the growth of a child's brain capacity and may interfere with his creativity and curiosity. He recommends that children up to ten years of age should be limited to one hour of TV a day, and even then it must be carefully monitored. Today there are excellent videos with great character examples distributed by Christian filmmakers. These are a good replacement for some of the TV viewing.

One young mother shared the story with me about how she was in the habit of keeping the TV set on all day long. She didn't really watch it but just had it on for "adult" company and conversation. Her 16-month-old baby was a perfectly healthy child except that he slept rather restlessly and was crankier than most babies. She decided one day to turn off the TV and not play it for long hours as she usually had. It had never occurred to her that there was any connection between the TV and her child's restlessness, but the child's behavior gradually began to change. He began to sleep better, he could concentrate on his own child's play much better, and he was much more contented. One psychologist says, "Television is too much noise, too much stimulation, and too much syncopation for a young child even if he is not watching."

Educators have been noticing a changing pattern of behavior in children, and they are attributing it to television. A schoolteacher commented that one little child had never walked normally at school. Every motion was exaggerated and slow-moving, an imitation of the then-popular "Six-Million-Dollar Man." This veteran teacher reported that there is an increase in children's shyness, passive behavior, and withdrawal, and they exhibit less creativity, imagination, and active involvement.

Too much television or videos robs a child of the enjoyment of good books. Television will never be an adequate substitute for the world of adventure found in children's books. But even though it is important for you to know that television may be hindering your child's intellectual development, I do not mean to say that TV should be banned completely. The decision depends on how carefully you screen all that he watches. Even though there are some excellent children's videos produced today that teach good morals, too much *good* TV or video time can hinder your child's individual creativity. Four is the age to put limits on TV time, before your child establishes a pattern that is hard to break later on.

The Choleric child is usually not excessively interested in TV. After all, it isn't productive. Choleric children hardly even like to play with the usual toys; they are much more interested in projects. Sanguines watch more TV but want someone to watch it with since they like to be around people. They occasionally wander in and out of the TV room to the cookie jar or to see what Mom is doing. The most TV watching is done by the Melancholic, who loses himself in what he watches and is affected by the emotion of the TV program. This is the child who will most likely try to mimic or reenact what he sees on television. The Phlegmatic will watch TV and sit glued to it until he gradually becomes bored and wanders off to do something else. He may even fall asleep in front of the television. Childish temperaments are unstable, so these TV reactions are not absolute, but they may alert you to the possible effects of TV on your child.

Spiritual Development

A child of this age needs to learn that God made everything around him—his lovable kitten, the delicious bananas, the cold water, and the beautiful flowers. As he becomes aware of things around him he will gradually realize that all good things come from God.

Some children become alert to spiritual matters more rapidly than others and begin to ask questions that could lead to their salvation very early. One of our daughters during this period had the traumatic experience of seeing her dog run over by a car. She began to question us if her little dog had gone to doggy heaven. We satisfied her by saying that God certainly must have a place for dogs of little girls.

Then she asked if *she* would go to heaven when she died. Because she asked such a straightforward question we very simply explained to her that she would, but first she would have to invite Jesus into her heart, and we explained why this was necessary. She responded, "I want to invite Jesus in right now." She prayed a very simple but meaningful prayer, and I firmly believe that on that day, at four years of age, she received Christ as her Lord and Savior.

Today she identifies that day as the time of her salvation. However, not every child will make a decision for Christ at that early age. It is important that you take each day a step at a time in leading your child to a vital relationship with Christ.

Books

Again I would like to stress the great value that books play in your child's life. Research has shown that the extent a child is read to during these early years correlates highly with his success in school. The preschooler needs to be read both fiction and nonfiction. Fiction increases his imagination and his creative thinking, while nonfiction gives him basic concepts that help him to understand his world and God.

A few books are listed below that I consider excellent material to be read to your child. This is a mere sampling of the vast array of books that are available. I suggest you visit your neighborhood library and your local Bible bookstore for a more complete list of books available.

Series of *I Can Read* books (Harper).
A Hole Is to Dig, by Ruth Krauss (Harper).
The Mr. Small Books, by Lois Lenski (Walck).
Horton Hatches an Egg, and others by Dr. Seuss (Random).
Fairest Lord Jesus, by Frances King Andrews (Broadman).
Everywhere I Go, by Dorothy Andrews (Christian Literature Crusade).
Little Visits with God, by Jahsmann and Simon (Concordia).

Seeing Progress

This has by no means been an exhaustive discussion of the four-year-old. It is simply intended to serve as an encouragement to what you are already doing right. These should be happy days for both parents and child, and if you follow sound, basic biblical principles for training, then this fourth year can well be a giant step in establishing stable parent-child relationships.

By now you have seen definite progress in your child's life from a totally helpless little infant to a youngster whose foundation is well-established for becoming a responsible adult. A good motto for the parents of four-year-olds can be: "Never do for your child what he can do for himself." Remember that at the end of this stage you will have helped your child develop about fifty percent of the intellectual potential he will ever have.

14

Skinned Knees and Schooldays

From this point onward children advance more distinctly as individuals. There will be overlapping of characteristics plus indefinite boundaries on different events in a child's life. In spite of this I have placed various topics in the general areas where you are most apt to meet them. Be flexible, and don't hold too rigidly to a development schedule.

Which School?

Sometimes Christian parents are only concerned that their children have a church relationship which will help them stay on the right track. This is critically important, but parents should not overlook the detrimental influence that a secular education could be having on their children. Too many children have been lovingly led to Christ at their parent's knee and then thrown to the potential destruction of the public school system. Wise parents will investigate the schools in their area. Meet the teachers and the principal, look at the textbooks, and even visit a few classes in different grade levels.

Also check out the private Christian schools in your area. If you live in a city where there is no choice of schools, then you need to counteract at home any negative influences that the school might have on your child. You should be aware that not all Christian schools meet satisfactory standards, just as all public schools do not. But today many Christian schools have improved to such a degree that they stand head and shoulders above public schools. Each one merits your investigation.

You may want to prayerfully consider a home-schooling program for your child. This is a growing educational movement that is showing tremendous success in educating Christian young people. I encourage you to check it out. I greatly appreciate the illustration given by Kenneth and Elizabeth Gangel in their book *Between Parent and Child*. They state that there are three influences on a child's life during the approximately 100 waking hours in a week. They are divided as follows:

School takes 35 to 40 hours a week.

Church and related ministries add five or six hours a week.

Home and parents have the remaining hours.

School occupies almost half of a child's waking hours each week. When all three of these influences agree on values and truths, they cooperate together in training the child. When one area of the three presents opposing views, then the other two must compensate with corrective training to counteract that opposition.

An Unknown World

Why do I present this subject for children of such a young age? Because the time to start proper educational training is at the very beginning, when a child is the most impressionable and easily influenced.

This is the time when many mothers go through an emotional shake-up as they realize that their young child is about to break out into the unknown world and that never again will there be the uninterrupted relationship between mother and child (unless, of course, she decides to teach him at home). Not only will she be sharing her child with a teacher who will greatly influence his life, but he will be gone from her care for as many as 20 to 30 hours a week. No wonder many a mother sheds a few tears on that first day of school when he leaves so excitedly to conquer his new world! Then one day, much later, the shock is almost too great when he challenges his parent's authority by saying, "But my teacher said this is the way to do it." Once again, you may want to investigate a home school possibility.

Some children develop real anxieties about separating from their mother and are afraid to start school. They may be eager when they leave the house, but by the time they get to school they are afraid because the teacher and the other children are strangers. This may cause a child to shrink back when the parent leaves him at the door of the school, and he may cling to Mom's legs for security. Reactions like this are most common among Phlegmatic and Melancholic children. There have been some very unpleasant and highly emotional scenes at the front door of many schools.

Most schools try to minimize this anxiety by inviting the child and parent to visit the school together before the child is left there alone. However, the best way to prepare the child to face this separation from home is for the parents to demonstrate a sensible attitude in preparing for that first day. A child who has started off as an infant attending the church nursery will be three steps ahead of a child who has never been to church. He has become familiar with the procedure that after a short separation from Mom and Dad, they always show up to claim him again. Young children who are accustomed to going out in public or having an occasional babysitter will be better able to adjust to the opening day of school.

The parent should never appear to be embarrassed, agitated, or angry regardless of how much commotion is made on the first day. It is a mistake for a parent to wait until the child is absorbed in play and then pull a disappearing act. The anxious child could conclude from this that the parent cannot be trusted. The wise response would be for the parent to encourage the child that everybody who starts school keeps going until the schoolday has finished.

Some mothers have suggested that it was easier for their child to leave them than for them to leave their child. If this is a possibility, you might prearrange with a high-school-aged friend to walk with him to school the first few days. That way he has left you at home; you have not left him at school.

The Temperament Response

You can probably expect that the Phlegmatic child will have the most difficult time making the break from home and adjusting to a strange new surrounding unless the parent has done a successful job of preparing him. He is just naturally more fearful anyway and will need the extra time required to prepare for that first day of school.

The Sanguine will be fine the minute he arrives and sees other children at school. Any fears he might have had will be immediately dismissed. In fact, he will probably be the one to comfort other fearful children who are hesitant to enter into the activities.

It will not be hard to spot the Choleric child on opening day. He will be there to give directions on what door to enter and be in full command of the slide or other playground equipment. Fear is not a part of his temperament. He knows that school is something you have to do, so you might as well do it and get it over with.

The Melancholic may experience some fear also. He will be slow to get involved in the group activities. He will be a little suspicious and may question the teacher several times if his mother is going to pick him up after school. His attention most likely will be drawn to something he can do quietly and all by himself. His mental attitude has to be properly prepared in order to help him want to go to school.

One of our children went through a difficult time when he started school. We had prepared him for months ahead to look forward to the beginning of school, and he did very well adjusting to the first three weeks. He would leave happily every day for school and then come home expressing his delight in his teacher and his new friends. However, after the first three weeks our family had to move, and he not only moved to a new home and new city, but to a new school as well. All the preparation we had built into him was now of no avail. It was a traumatic experience for him. There were a lot of tears and much pleading. We probably didn't handle it as well as we could have because of our involvement in a major move, but with much love and patience we tried to give him a sense of new security, and he gradually overcame the trauma. Today he is a grown man, and it appears that this experience did not leave a permanent scar on him.

On the brighter side, in most cases the distress that a child experiences at the beginning of school, even though it might be troublesome, is a very normal occurrence and does not indicate a disturbed child.

Mental Growth

It is very exciting when your first-grader begins to recognize words and simple sentences in print and develops a real feeling of accomplishment through this. (When he is in third grade he will have developed a wider vocabulary and will be able to read aloud for others.)

The academic accomplishments during these years are fantastic. He will move from very little knowledge to a working knowledge about math, reading, writing, science, and spelling. He is full of curiosity and enthusiasm for learning. Experts tell us that 80 percent of his capacity for learning will have been developed by the time he is eight years old. Expose him to many opportunities for learning. He is very responsive to intellectual stimulation and should be challenged and stimulated to increase his capacity. Don't underestimate his capabilities!

Physical Growth

This primary child has now gained more poise and muscular skills. He wants to do things himself instead of just watching others do them. Don't expect him to sit still very long; his interest span is still rather limited. His muscles seem to tire when he is in one position too long, and this causes him to wiggle and squirm. He is young and active, but he tires easily; therefore he should be in bed at an early hour in order to get sufficient rest. His limited television viewing should not be made up of violence or frightening programs which would cause him to have nightmares or restless nights. In fact, the less TV he watches, the better he will be able to completely relax in his bed.

He seems to have spurts of growth. The most common remark from mothers of this age is that they can't keep their children in shoes or clothes because of their rapid growth. His greatest growth is in his arms and legs, which makes him taller and thinner.

The most frequent trademark of children of this age is their toothless grin and uneven teeth. Large teeth will be growing next to small teeth. It is very obvious that he has come a long way during these few years.

Spiritual Growth

A child of this age has a rapidly growing concept of God and may be ready to accept Christ as his Savior. The parent should be sensitive to the questions he asks about God, heaven, death, or sin. Be careful not to force the child to make a decision about something he does not understand. Not all children at this age are ready to receive Christ. In this case, continue leading him to understand more about God and Jesus. However, if you feel he is ready and understands what he is doing, then by all means lead him to invite Jesus into his heart. He must understand that it is only because of God's love that he can be forgiven of his sins.

He usually loves Sunday school and looks forward to Sundays as the best day of the week. However, the attitude that the parents have toward Sunday school and church will gradually be adopted by the child, whether it is positive or negative. Church should be a family experience where Mom and Dad take the children with them to church. The child should be challenged to memorize Bible verses, but they should be verses that he can understand and can translate into everyday experience.

Special Training

There are several areas where a child needs special training during this stage. One is training in basic social behaviors. Young children are not automatically courteous. This comes only by training, and I encourage parents to spend adequate time teaching common courtesy to their child. Too many children are growing into adulthood today without the faintest idea of how to be polite and good-mannered. They want everyone to listen to them when they talk, but not the other way around. Yet with training they will learn courtesy in listening to others also. The three important words to stress at this age are "please," "thank you," and "excuse me."

The most effective training is through practicing politeness and respect in the home. When the parent and child make a habit of practicing courteous habits at home, then it is much easier for both of them to behave this way in other situations as well.

Your child should be encouraged to share his possessions, since he may tend to be selfish. He needs to learn how to "give and take." Even though he may have a temperament that is naturally generous, he will tend to go through a stage of selfishness at this time. He is still the center of his own universe, and he needs to be taught that he cannot always be first or have the most or the best.

Temper tantrums are usually over by this age, but if he is a Sanguine or Melancholic, he may still occasionally lose his temper. The child who responds to punishment with an angry explosion definitely needs some strong measures of discipline.

Probably the most frequently asked question in our seminars is "What do you do with a little child that cries out in anger after a spanking?" or as they say in South Africa, "after a hiding." After one seminar in South Africa I had eight different sets of parents line up after the meeting to ask advice on how to cope with their child who responded to a "hiding" with a fit of anger. My answer for dealing with a child this age is to finish the spanking for the disobedience; then, when it is obvious that he is screaming in rage and not in hurt or embarrassment, go to him and speak in a calm, medium voice. DO NOT BE ANGRY! Tell him that his punishment is over for the original disobedience and that you have forgiven him. And now you want to forget it.

But his outburst of rage is another problem that has to be dealt with. If you can say it honestly, then tell him that Mom and Dad do not burst out in anger like this and that your home is going to be a place of peace and harmony. So the second punishment is for the fit of rage. It should be strong enough to send a signal to his brain that his outburst of anger is painful and will not be worth it the next time. This may have to be repeated many times, but eventually he will get the message that this anger is not acceptable. Believe me, you will be glad you dealt with this now rather than waiting until he becomes a teen or an adult.

When the anger is passed and the storm is over, it would be good to involve him in a discussion on what the Bible says about anger. Keep it simple so he can understand it, but he needs to know that you have the Word of God to back you up. It will be worthless to share this while he is in the midst of his rage. Proverbs 19:18,19 says, "Chasten your son while there is hope, and do not set your heart on his destruction. A man of great wrath shall suffer punishment; for if you deliver him, you will have to do it again."

Much of his behavior will be determined by what he thinks of himself. When a boy thinks he is "bad," he usually acts that way; if a girl thinks she is "stupid," she will probably do things that make her appear stupid. It is important for parents to build up the child's self-image by refraining from ridiculing, criticizing, or tearing him down. When he has done something that is worthy of an acceptable comment from you, be sure you give it. You build his self-acceptance and confidence by the way you let him know that you approve of and accept him. Dads especially need to work at commending their son or daughter for an act well done. It means more to your child than you can imagine.

If your son or daughter still has problems with bed-wetting, by all means do not punish or shame him. Most likely he is already embarrassed and ashamed. He may be a sound sleeper and not aware of his impulses that tell him to go to the bathroom. He will be embarrassed and humiliated and will need your love instead of criticism and disapproval. Don't even show exasperation. Let him know that you fully understand and would like to make it a team effort to help him overcome this challenge in his life. You may want to teach him how to handle his own sheets and pajamas by gathering them and putting them in the washing machine each day.

Special Traits

This is the age when children are not as repulsed by the opposite sex as they will be in a couple of years. In fact they like the opposite sex. Little boys often love little girls and even decide which one they will marry when they grow up. A boy likes to talk about his girlfriend at this age and even boast to others how many times he has kissed her. But as he becomes older, his talk will change because he doesn't want to be teased. He will think girls are "silly" and won't even sit next to them. Girls will have the same reaction against boys.

This is the age of meaningful questions. The best form of sex education is to answer the questions as they are asked. Answer them openly, directly, honestly, and matter-of-factly. If you avoid discussing these topics with your child, he can get the idea that you do not approve of this subject because it is "dirty" or "forbidden." You should be the one to inform him of the facts of life to be sure that the information he is getting is accurate and that it is built around lessons on morality. Even at this young age he will hear about sex from his more "worldly-wise" peers.

A book I recommend for parents is the one that Tim and I recently wrote, *Against the Tide* (Questar Publishers), with the subtitle "How to Raise Sexually Pure Kids in an 'Anything-Goes' World." If you have questions or are troubled about how to handle this extremely important subject with your growing child, then this book has the answers for you. (I encourage *both* parents to read it.) It is important to get started right in unfolding this new dimension of life for your child.

Good Books

No doubt by now you are getting the message of what I believe about books for your children. Hopefully you are already well-established in the habit of reading together. As your child develops in this stage, he will want to begin reading for himself. Encourage his desire. Go with him to the library, being careful that he doesn't bring home books that are too hard for him to read. Our own children were excited to read books by themselves, but we still included the "reading together" time, which involved several members of the family. In this way they were still able to experience the adventure of books that were beyond their own reading skills.

You may begin to find that your child's response to listening or reading may be influenced by his temperament. The Sanguine will want to flit from the first chapter to the last to quickly see how the story ends. He may tend to be restless and would rather be outside playing with his friends. Your encouragement will help keep him listening. You may find that he easily cries with sad stories and laughs at funny ones.

The Choleric would also rather be out playing ball instead of reading or listening. However, the kind of stories you select will keep his interest if they are packed with action and adventure and you can involve him in the story somehow. Once he learns to read, even a little, he would rather try to read by himself than be read to.

It is the Melancholic who will most enjoy story time. He will probably want to sit right on top of you as you read to him and will become personally involved in each character.

The Phlegmatic will be willing to sit for long periods of time with a good book. If the story doesn't interest him, he will still sit quietly, but may slip off into daydreaming.

The range of books is very long for a child of this age, but I would like to list a few of our family's favorites. Any public library can help you check out a regular supply of books.

Winnie the Pooh, by A.A. Milne (Dutton).
The House on Pooh Corner, by A.A. Milne (Dutton).
The Story of Ferdinand, by Munro Leaf (Viking).

Five Chinese Brothers, by Claire H. Bishop (Coward).
The Madeline Book Series, by Ludwig Bemelmans (Viking).
Richard's Bible Story Book (Zondervan).
Egermeier's Bible Story Book (Moody Press).

There are many more excellent books. Browse through your local Christian bookstore and see for yourself the vast number of choices before you.

It is vitally important for parents to be alert to their child's reading ability. Watch for the improvement of his skills. By the third grade he should be able to read smoothly with expression and comprehension. Ask him to read to you from time to time, and show real interest in his achievement.

It may be that he will need supplemental help during the first two years. If he doesn't learn to read well, this will put limits on him as he pursues a life's profession. More than that, it will affect his everyday standard of living. Remember, you are what you read!

15

Roller Blades and Primping

Your child's next few years will be characterized by an interesting conflict between fighting with their friends and then sticking up for them, between hating the opposite sex and then primping for them, and between hating school and then enjoying it. These years are filled with energy, enthusiasm, arguing, and learning.

Any parent with a child of this age will be able to enjoy his young boy or girl more if he learns to relax and flex with the child's changing moods. You may need to laugh with or at him occasionally. Be careful that you don't let yourself mentally think of him as a complex human being. He is young and is struggling to get past this stage of growth. If you have already determined the temperament, it will help you to understand why her room is always messy, why he spends so much time in the principal's office, why he wants to wear his hair like he does, why she has scraps with her best girlfriends, or why he wears his loose, sloppy clothes when he gets dressed up.

How you learn to enjoy and guide your children in the midst of these extremes and aggravations will determine to a great extent how you relate to them as teenagers. Carefully choose your areas of conflict. There will be some things that are not important enough to make a big fuss about. Be an encouragement to your children and build them up. You will be building on the foundation that you laid a few years back.

Learning: Burden or Benefit?

School is a necessity but can be such a burden to some junior children. Your child's temperament will play an important role in his attitude toward school. When the school bell rings at the close of the day, some students will race out the door like the building was on fire, while others will linger long after school is dismissed.

The Sanguine and Choleric will knock each other over getting out the door. In fact, they will probably be out of the building before the bell has stopped ringing. It's not that they are so eager to get home to their mother, but that they are both lovers of sports and competition and can hardly wait to reach the playground or ball field after school. The Sanguine will enjoy any activity of play as long as there are other kids around. When they start to leave, he will too. But the Choleric will be the last to leave, especially if there are organized activities. He has a driving compulsion to be a winner and will want to play longer to get a chance to win or to win again. Neither of these temperaments is too concerned about tomorrow's homework assignment.

The Melancholic will linger after the bell for many reasons. For one, it is highly possible that he or she will be infatuated with the teacher and will want to stay longer to help and be near her. He is eager to wash blackboards, clean erasers, or any number of other things. There is also the concern that he might forget an assignment, so he finds it necessary to go over all this with the teacher again. And of course he will take every book home just to be sure he has the right one.

The slowest one to leave may be the Phlegmatic. He will start to clean out his desk after the bell has rung. His desk will be straightened and reorganized over and over again. Then when he finally leaves school he will poke all the way home. He will kick every pebble and pet every dog and cat. When he finally arrives home he will remember that he forgot to bring his assignment with him.

Regardless of his attitude to get out of school at the end of the day, every child at this age should be stimulated to study and to think. He should be challenged to do some real thinking. When he asks questions, it will be most beneficial if the parent would guide his thinking so he can discover the answer for himself rather than just give him the answer.

Help him to establish good study habits, especially the Sanguine or Phlegmatic, who will tend to procrastinate and dillydally around. Provide him with an atmosphere and the equipment for study. When the TV is blaring and the family is yelling across the house, it is difficult for any human being to study. Parents should never do the work for the child, but should show a genuine interest in the homework and be able to discuss it together. The child will be impressed and challenged when the parent is interested in what he is studying.

Bettering Reading Skills

Most boys and girls of this age love to read, and the wise parent will encourage it. He may enter this stage as a slow reader, but his reading skills should develop rapidly, enabling him to read with speed and comprehension. Any encouragement or tutoring the parent can give to better the child's reading skills will benefit him for the rest of his life.

We were fortunate to live close to a public library during these crucial years in our children's lives. This library ran a three-month summer reading program for the neighborhood kids. It was very competitive, and junior boys and girls love competition, whether it is in sports or reading. A large chart was posted inside the library door with the name of every kid who entered the reading program, and each week the number of books he finished was posted for all the world to see. The program required that each competitor read at least two books a week to stay in the competition, and they had designed a clever, comprehensive report to determine if the child had read the book and understood it.

One summer our children read so many books that I finally had to limit the amount of time each day they could read in order to keep a proper balance. But their reading skills and vocabularies increased with great strides. It is important that the child at this age does not read to escape reality. If he feels inferior to his playmates, he may retreat to the security of a book. Thus it is wise to keep a good balance for his proper development.

Reading opens up new areas of interest. Reading helps boys and girls become more interested and informed in science, famous people, history, geography, Bible stories, etc. Books help to broaden the horizons of each young reader. I firmly believe that books become more interesting to any child when the TV is limited in the home. Books and TV mix about as well as oil and water. Good books will stimulate any person's imagination and creative abilities.

There are many good books that juniors should be familiar with. In fact, there are so many that it is virtually impossible to list them all. A reliable list of excellent books for all ages is found in Gladys Hunt's book *Honey for a Child's Heart* (Zondervan). It is a guidebook on both secular and Christian books for parents to consult regarding reading material for each age. Probably at the head of any list would be the seven children's books by C.S. Lewis; the first in the series is titled *The Lion, The Witch, and The Wardrobe.*

All Play and No Work?

It seems that energy is wasted on youth, since all a child wants to do is play. How often adults wish they could bottle up some of this boundless energy for the more productive years! The junior boy or girl can work very hard at playing, but he hates it if you ask him to work. I watched several boys "play" very hard to clear a portion of snow off the ice for skating. If their fathers had asked them to shovel the snow off the sidewalk that would have been called "work" and they would have begrugdingly done it.

Juniors are full of energy and need direction and guidance so that their energy is used constructively and not destructively. It is remarkable how quickly their zeal fades when they are asked to do the dinner dishes! But subtle motivation may stimulate them to first get the job done and then do something they find more enjoyable. A possible suggestion: "After we're finished with the dishes I'll challenge you to a game of Monopoly" (or whatever the family game or hobby is at your house). Give them a goal to reach beyond the unpleasant task they must do.

Sin is Sin

This child is now old enough to recognize that sin is sin, and he will feel the guilt that it produces. Some children have already received Christ by the time they enter the fourth grade, but statistics show that more people accept Christ during these years than at any other time in life. Their hearts are ready and they sense the need for help in overcoming their temptations.

If Mom and Dad have laid the proper groundwork during the previous stage, then it should be very normal for the junior to receive Christ during this period of life. The parents' attitude toward Sunday school, church, and Jesus Christ during his junior years will be reflected by him when he reaches junior high. When a parent stays home from church every time a "Sunday headache" occurs or his favorite team is playing football on TV, the junior boy or girl will begin to capture the same spirit.

Since this is such an important stage in the spiritual life of a young person, it is vital that the Sunday school provide the very best motivation. The most capable and Spirit-filled leader in the Sunday school should be in charge of the junior department. Dr. Henrietta Mears, a well-known Christian educator and motivational speaker of the past, and especially known for building successful Sunday schools, once said that a junior should not be graduated out of the department without the opportunity to receive Christ. Every teacher in this department should be committed to this goal. Woe unto the teacher who is careless and negligent to pray and prepare for that important hour each week that he has to influence a junior's life!

The child's education regarding Jesus Christ and the Christian life can best be done in the home and should be started at an early age. Then it becomes a normal acceptance of spiritual concepts and he adapts them to his own life. Your prayers and faithful teaching, including his Sunday school training, will lead him to an early acceptance of Jesus Christ as Savior.

Family Worship

Family worship is a very valuable part of training the children, but in too many homes it has become a very formal and stiff period of time after the evening meal that the whole family looks at with boredom. There is nothing spiritual in sounding the gong and announcing, "Family worship will now begin!" Since the Bible does not tell us how family training should be accomplished, why not use a little imagination and give it variety and interest?

I suggest that family devotions be a very natural and informal time, with everybody participating. Does it have to be after the evening meal each time? Let it be a planned discussion during the meal that is instigated by Dad with everyone participating, and then Dad concludes with God's words. This can be practical, interesting, and geared to any age level. The junior boy or girl especially enjoys this type of devotion because it is not all listening and he can be involved in it. This can be a great time for teaching practical Christian living to your children.

Special Traits

The junior child usually feels rather awkward about an open display of affection. He wants to be loved and needs to be loved, but don't overdo it, especially with the boys. When Aunt Mamie comes to visit and plants a big kiss and hug on junior, it causes him to do all sorts of funny things. We had one son who seemed to disappear when certain people came to visit us. He could not handle any outward show of affection to him at this stage in life.

Rather than make your child stand there and allow Aunt Mamie to embarrass and humiliate him, treat his response nonchalantly. If he chooses to disappear for awhile, don't go in his room and drag him out. Sooner or later he will be curious about what is going on in the other room and will slip back into the room unnoticed and blend into the family activities. Forcing him to react contrary to his emotions will only make a bigger issue of the situation than necessary.

Moms and dads should still display love and affection to their junior son, but should do it discreetly. Some boys don't seem to mind such a public display of parental affection, but if your son does, don't insist on kissing him goodbye in front of the school when you drop him off in the morning. Keep your kisses for that goodnight hug in the privacy of his bedroom. My husband would faithfully go into the bedroom of our sons, pull the covers around their neck, and tell them that he loved them as he tenderly placed a goodnight kiss on their head or cheek. But outside in public they seemed to understand each other, and goodbye was just a touch on the shoulder or a pat on the back.

Girls don't seem to struggle with this as much as boys. Our girls seemed to be much better at coping with love and affection in public. Here again the temperament plays an important role in how your daughter responds to affection, as does the foundation you have laid prior to this age. Every girl needs to feel free to sit on her father's lap and put her arms around his neck. This is the best preparation a girl can have for becoming a responsive, loving wife. If a junior girl does not have a warm, open relationship with her father, then it may be difficult for her to have a loving relationship with a marriage partner.

Junior boys usually think girls are "silly" and "stupid," and junior girls think boys are "show-offs" and "pests." For many years I was in charge of the junior department in our Sunday school. One absolutely distinctive characteristic I noticed was that junior boys did not want to sit in the same row with junior girls, and vice versa. In fact, the greatest competition and friendly rivalry in contests and Bible drills came from putting boys on one team and girls on the other.

Dislike of the opposite sex promotes a greater spirit of love for the "group," particularly with boys. They like to do things in a bunch rather than singularly. There is a real spirit of loyalty between boys that are in the same clique—more so than with girls. Girls at this age seem to get into scraps and not get along too well together. They will sometimes even pick a fight with their best friends.

It is wise for the parent to be observant but not involved in these girlish skirmishes, unless the situation gets out of hand. Usually the girl she fought with last week will become her bosom buddy within a few days. The Choleric and Melancholic girls are most likely to be disagreeable with their best friends.

A Demand for Fairness

The demand for fairness is a natural characteristic of a junior child. If something appears to be off-sided, he will quickly respond with "That's just not fair." He recognizes injustice, so be ready and willing to admit it when you have dealt with him unfairly. Be willing to ask his forgiveness.

Years ago my husband had punished one of our sons for a deed and then it became apparent that he had punished the wrong son. When a parent realizes this, he must be willing to confess the wrong to the child and ask his forgiveness. It isn't enough to just say, "Well, that serves him right for all the times he should have been punished and wasn't." My husband admitted his wrong to the boy and asked his forgiveness. Our son looked his dad square in the eye and said, "Of course, Dad, I realize that you're not perfect!"

Many years later, while speaking with my husband at a Family Life Seminar, I told this story, and our son, now grown and the father of two boys, was present in the meeting. Afterward he said to us, "Dad, that's strange. I don't remember that spanking you gave me." My husband turned to me and said, "Honey, you can be sure he would have remembered it if I had not asked his forgiveness." How valuable it is to deal fairly, squarely, and honestly with our children. They can handle parental mistakes if you are open and truthful with them.

What About Appearances?

Very few junior boys care how they look. Their hair can be tousled, their shoes unlaced, their shirts hanging out, their pants loose and baggy, with dirt smudges where they have wiped their hands. Their shirts may be dirty and wrinkled, but if it is their favorite, they will want to wear it again. Perhaps the Phlegmatic will be an exception to this because he is basically neat and tidy. However, at this age even he can be different. But all the temperaments need to be encouraged to care for their own belongings and to have a neat appearance.

A junior's room is usually a disaster area if left alone. One parent related the story to me about her daughter. Her room was continuously in a disorganized mess, with clothes left just where she had taken them off. One evening while everyone was away, their burglar alarm sounded and the police arrived. Moments later, the college-age son came home and found the police walking around the outside of the house. They quickly explained that the alarm had sounded and one policeman said, "I think I found the room where they entered. It looks like it has been ransacked." The policeman led them around to the window of the girl's room and they all peered in. Sure enough, it *did* look like it had been ransacked, but the son said, "No, her room always looks like that!" It was a false alarm, and the officers went away chuckling to themselves.

This is an area where parents need to motivate and encourage their children to improve. Nagging will not do it! It will take teamwork between parent and child to get him going and help him know how to do it. He will generally want to do it by himself, but if he knows that you are going to come and assist him, that will usually motivate him to clean up his own mess.

At the close of this stage you may begin to see traces of change appearing. The boys will start to linger a little longer in front of the mirror. Girls will take a little more care to see that their hair is curled and their clothes are looking just right. And one day soon you will wake up to the fact that the bathroom mirror is always in use. It will either be the son primping or the daughter drying and curling her hair. What brought about the change? Sorry, Mom, you may think it was your excellent training, but it is simply that they have discovered the opposite sex in a new light!

Handling Money

An integral part of a child's training is teaching him how to manage money. Many parents start even earlier, but certainly by this stage you need to have a definite plan in operation to teach your child the value of money and how to manage it. As he learns this, he will also be learning how to make judgments, accept the consequence of his judgments, and live with the problems he creates.

1. *Give him a regular allowance.* The allowance should be a follow-up to assigned chores. This is a great way to teach a work ethic. After all, in the real world money is received only when you have worked for it. Set an exact amount (not too little or too much). I have been appalled at the amount some children are being given for a weekly allowance and for no specific reason. Whatever you decide, it should be paid on the same day each week, perhaps every Saturday. Discuss with him what expenses his allowance is to cover. Start by teaching him to set aside 10 percent every week for his gift to the Lord. This is the first lesson in tithing. I would suggest that you schedule a limited amount to cover his special treats. Then another percentage should be set aside for a savings account. If he wants to purchase a more expensive item, he will learn that he needs to plan and save for it. By doing this you will have started your child on a path of wise financial planning and spending.

2. *Don't punish with money.* Money should not be confused with power or love. It is essential to keep praise and reproof separate from financial transactions.

3. *Let him make mistakes.* Spending money means making choices, and everyone is bound to make a mistake from time to time. Don't automatically bail him out, but offer empathy and guidance. However, if he has really gone in over his head, you may need to extend him a loan that he will pay back to you from future allowances. But set it up in a businesslike arrangement.

4. *Teach sensible saving.* Rather than encouraging him to save just for the sake of saving, suggest that he save toward a specific goal, such as a new bicycle. A junior will not be too excited about saving for a college education. That is too remote for him, so start with a goal that he can achieve in the near future.

5. *Encourage him to tithe.* Regardless of how little the tithe might be, it is teaching a very valuable lesson to your child. When he learns to cheerfully give 10 percent of his meager allowance to the Lord at this age, it becomes easier to give more as he grows older.

Each temperament will respond to money in different ways, and the early allowance will help your child profit from his mistakes. The Sanguine will be an impulsive spender; the Choleric will be the most practical with his money (he may want to start with simple investments); the Melancholic will be indecisive, and when he does spend his money he may have buyers' remorse; the Phlegmatic will be stingy and save it all for himself. It is good for the parent to observe how each child handles his money and then guide him to better management.

Sex Education

Even though a form of sex education for your child has been going on for several years now, he is approaching the age for more serious questions. If he is not asking any, it may be that he is getting his answers on the playground. In this case you would be wise to naturally direct the conversation to a few leading questions of your own.

It is far better for your child to have the straight facts from his parents than to get the playground interpretation.

A fine book for parents to share with their child when he reaches this stage is *Almost Twelve*, by Kenneth Taylor (Tyndale Publishers). This book gives a simple but complete description of human reproduction as God designed it to be. This book has been around for several years, but the basic facts of morality have not changed. The book I referred to in the last chapter, *Against the Tide: How to Raise Sexually Pure Kids in an "Anything-Goes"World,* would be a great help in raising a child of this age as well. There is an entire section dedicated to teaching your junior-age boy and girl about sex. I recommend it for every parent to read.

You need to prepare yourself with the facts before you can prepare your child. He needs to learn the basics about sex education and have it interwoven with strong moral principles. Unfortunately, today's young person is gaining a knowledge about sex that has little to do with moral values. Parents need to be involved with their children's sex education. Just before they enter junior high, it is wise for them to know that the pleasures of intercourse can have serious consequences. God has designed it to be reserved *only* for marriage.

Family Unity

This can be a fun age. Your children are now old enough to interact with you in discussions, in work, and in playing games. This time will be what you make it. I have to chuckle inside when I hear my kids, who are now grown, tell others that we have always had a family tradition to do certain

things. And they will proudly name several. Some of them I
had forgotten about, and I didn't even realize others were
traditions. But they have left impressions on our children,
and now they are proudly labeled as "our family traditions."

Families are drawn together in a beautiful unity by
things that may be called "tradition" but were really created out of love and fellowship during this fun junior stage.

16

The Tough and Tender Years

To children there is nothing more exciting than their thirteenth birthdays. (To the parents it is often terrifying!) This day signals their first steps into the adult world. When they start developing physically (if they haven't already), they will accelerate the long process of becoming independent. This is a period of time in every child's life when they need more involvement with their parents, not less.

But you should not be starting now. The starting time for parental involvement should be at the very beginning. Unfortunately, there is a tendency for parents to start backing off when their child reaches the teen years because they feel that their parenting days are beginning to taper off. Not so! This is a critical time for you to build on what you have started. Walking with your child through the next five years could be the deciding factor in his destruction or success.

No other period of life is stormier than the teen years, not just for the parents but for the teenager himself. One minute he acts like a child, the next he feels like an adult.

Cholerics want their independence before any other temperaments, then Sanguines, then Melancholics, and finally Phlegmatics. As one authority said in pointing out the difference in teens, "Some 13-year-old girls are excellent babysitters, while others at 13 still need a babysitter themselves."

At the entrance to the teen years, your child's sex is often more distinguishing than his temperament. It is well-known that girls tend to be more mature at this age than boys, not only physically but also mentally and emotionally. This accounts for girls' greater interest in the opposite sex and for their attraction to older boys. This differing maturation level usually evens out between 20 and 23. But don't expect a change in temperament; you will find that your teenager manifests the same basic personality traits he had when he was little, except now they take on larger and more adult proportions.

If you did your parental homework when your children were small, raising teenagers can be real fun. But if you wasted the opportunities to bond with them while molding their character and enriching their temperament when they were young, you will have your work cut out for you during the next six years of life. James Dobson has aptly stated, "The time to disarm that teenage time bomb is before he is five years old."

A number of years ago, as my husband and I drove home after an evening of fellowship with friends whose preschool children sassed their parents and rebelliously threw their weight around most of the night, he remarked, "These folks are going to have a heartache on their hands ten or twelve years from now." And I'm sorry to report that he was right. Parents need to start much earlier, well before the teen years, to get control over who is the parent and who is the child.

Why All the Conflict?

Entrance into the teen years is not only exciting to the teenager, but it can be downright terrifying to him at the same time. It often means going to junior high school (where he starts out on the bottom as a seventh-grader after being a big-shot sixth-grader the year before) with new friends, new challenges, and new faces. The opposite sex becomes more attractive and desirable. Soon he goes to high school and even expects the keys to the family car. After that he goes away to college, enters the work force, or marries. In short, the prospect of adulthood can be frightening because it requires the one thing all human beings are most afraid of—change.

The most significant changes that young teenagers face are physical and sexual. The innocence of childhood is suddenly replaced by sexual feelings that inspire guilt. Girls often have amorous sensations, causing the first boy-crazy stage that embarrasses both their parents and themselves. During a summer after graduating from sixth grade, one of our girls looked out the window of the church and recognized a budding ninth-grade girlfriend she had long admired and said, "Ugh! I'm ashamed of Sarah. She is out there batting her eyelashes at the boys." Two years later I looked out the window to see our daughter doing exactly the same thing!

Fathers often forget and mothers cannot understand the trauma a boy feels when he experiences his first erection, or the shame and embarrassment he feels after his first nocturnal emission. The Sanguine or Choleric boy will find out from his peers what made him wake up "in a mess." The Melancholic or Phlegmatic will usually keep such experiences to himself and will carry unnecessary guilt for a protracted period of time.

Because of the guilt feelings associated with their emerging sex drives, don't be surprised if your teenagers begin to avoid showing affection to the parent of the opposite sex. This is usually a temporary period, but it is very important that they be assured of your love during that time. They don't feel worthy of your love, but they want it and need it more than ever. Unfortunately, their behavior makes it difficult to love them—but love them anyway. The late Henrietta C. Mears, a lady who greatly influenced my husband and me, and who was a great youth worker in her day, used to say, "At this stage of life only the parents can love them, and sometimes the father wonders how the mother can stand them."

Feelings of Insecurity

Another reason for conflict is the intense feelings of inferiority and insecurity which early teenagers experience. As they enter this preadult world, they are usually conscious of their ineptitude, inexperience, and insufficiency. Yet they have a real desire for acceptance. Consequently, they may act rebellious when you treat them like a child because they cannot perform tasks on an adult level. During this stage they need understanding, instruction, and encouragement, but not constant criticism. Parental approval is worth more than we often realize.

Try to avoid showing your exasperation when your teenager fouls things up. Remember what he was like just a couple of years before. He is certainly not mature yet, and it is unfair to expect performance beyond his capabilities. It is also important that you see your teenager as he is going to be someday: mature, dependable, and capable. If you think of him as inept, lazy, clumsy, etc., you will emote that message to him even if you don't say a word about it. That only confirms his feelings of inadequacy, particularly in the Melancholic, the Phlegmatic, and sometimes the Sanguine.

Keep in mind the quest for recognition as your child grows every day after his thirteenth birthday. Your approval, whenever it is possible to give it honestly, will offer hope that he will someday make it. If you don't believe in him, he certainly isn't going to believe in himself. If you view him as a loser, he will probably be a loser, but if you see him as a winner and let him know that, he will work harder toward being a winner. It is a known fact that the most important people in assisting an early teenager to accept himself are his parents.

Desire for Freedom

Another thing that accelerates teenage/parent conflicts all through these growing years is the teenager's desire for more freedom before his parents think he is ready for it. The parent feels, "Show me you're responsible and I'll increase your privileges." The teen says, "Give me more privileges and I'll show you I'm responsible." One of the complaints I often hear from teenagers is "My parents don't trust me." Yet often it isn't a matter of trust; it is simply immaturity. The teenager thinks he is more adult than do his mother and father.

Most parents should give their teenagers more adult responsibilities than they do, but it should be made clear that future opportunities depend on present performance. Parents have a right to expect their teenager to take reasonable care of his clothes, room, homework, and other normal assignments in order to earn more adult privileges. It is impossible to give pat answers on when to "let go" and when to "hang on," but when a young person acts like an adult, he should be treated like one. Of course, the opposite is also true. The important factor is to be realistic in your expectations.

The Four F's

To this day our family (including those married and raising their own children) still refer to "the Four F's." It has always meant "family, fun, food, and fellowship." Teenagers often have lots of energy—except for work—and now that they are getting bigger, they can engage in more adult activities. Develop family traditions, activities, hobbies, sports, vacations, etc. that you can enjoy together as a family. Take your teenagers on picnics or outings, play games with them, and let them compete with you. It may take a lot of your time during a six-to-twelve-year period of your life, depending on how many children you have, but it will save you many heartaches later.

Today's lifestyle offers people more leisure time than for any previous generation in the history of the world. Much of that time should be spent together as a family, but be sure to learn to do things that appeal to both teenagers and adults. Sometimes that means teaching the young people something you enjoy, and at times it may mean doing things to please them which may not be your favorite pastimes.

When our children were young, my husband gave up golfing for water skiing with the family (he decided he didn't have time for both). The whole family participated in this family sport. When the kids were young, I learned to drive the boat because it was a "Family Four F" event. Little did we realize that we were gaining an activity that we could do together on vacations, even after grandchildren came along. The grandchildren started their first water ski lessons between three and four years of age. (The kids say that one requirement to marry into our family is the ability to water ski or a willingness to learn!) Now, more than two decades later, every year our family has spent a week together, children and grandchildren, on a water skiing vacation at Lake Powell. It is truly a family tradition that keeps our family very close.

Ever since I've known him, my husband has been a football fanatic. At first I wasn't much interested in football, but instead of opposing him over it I decided to join him. Now I enjoy football almost as much as he does. When the children became teenagers, we made a family event out of football. I would prepare a picnic basket, and since we could only afford general admission tickets, we all went early and stood in line to be sure we got good seats.

We were fortunate enough to live in a city that had a professional football team. Each game provided five or six hours of "family, fun, food, and fellowship." The record book shows that the San Diego Chargers did not always do too well in the ratings, but our family scored high in family togetherness. All through those years we had holiday "Four F's" at our home throughout the TV football season. In addition to these activities, as our children got older we took up snow skiing. Little did we dream in those early days that our children would grow up one day to be our best friends.

Speaking of friends, all temperaments have friends, even the Melancholic youth, although he usually limits them to one or two. One way to keep your children from running around with young people you don't approve of is to make your home a haven for their friends and let them invite their friends along on some of your "Four F" outings. Subconsciously they will select friends their family approves of. In fact, if your children are close enough in age, you won't have to say much when one of them invites someone who isn't a good influence on him; the brothers and sisters will point it out, sometimes quite painfully.

Athletics As a Tool

Today's physical fitness craze has people jogging, cycling, climbing, snorkeling, hiking, and a host of other things we never thought of as teens. Those who know say this craze is with us to stay, so you might as well use it as a tool. In their quest for their own individuality, it is important that your teens learn to do many things and that they do at least one thing well.

Every teen wants to be popular. Have you ever noticed that the kids who have many friends usually can do most anything, or because they do so many things, they are not afraid to try others? The girl that can water ski respectably, play miniature golf without losing her ball, and play a decent game of tennis rarely lacks dates in high school. Boys today don't go much for wallflowers who are afraid to try something new. You may never be an expert at any of these things, but you can learn to enjoy them. And you can encourage your teens to learn. It is important for their development.

Dr. Dobson points out that each child must learn to excel at something. It helps him to gain much-needed self-acceptance. Accomplishment in one area of life will give him confidence in others. Find out what your teen has an affinity for and get him to take lessons and practice consistently, if possible. If sports is not his interest, then try a musical instrument, band, hobbies, or something else. They need to learn expertise in at least one area of life. Unless your child is a natural-born athlete (which can happen to any temperament), you may find that his own temperament and his peer group will often determine his desire for sports.

Sanguines are enthusiastic about everything, so they try their hand at every activity. Unfortunately, their lack of discipline makes it difficult for them to keep at a sport after it loses its novelty, and their restlessness inspires them to try something else. Consequently, they often know how to do a lot of things, but excel at none. Parental encouragement to keep at it during the drudgery stage, encountered in learning any sport, can well make the difference for the Sanguine.

The Choleric child is a natural competitor and is often consumed by sports. He may letter in four sports and show little interest in dating or in scholastics all through high school.

The Phlegmatic youth needs constant encouragement to get involved with other young people. He is not usually assertive and resists competition. Although well-coordinated and basically capable, he rarely takes advantage of his potential. But once he gains confidence in his ability in a certain sport, he goes on to be above average. Phlegmatics are often drawn to the individual sports, such as tennis, track, or swimming. If, however, his peers are involved in a group sport, he may well put out the extra effort to excel in that also. Parental encouragement without nagging will make the difference.

Melancholic young people fall into one of two categories: Either they are very good at sports and excelling comes easy for them, or, more commonly, they show little or no interest or aptitude for sports. No one can be more antisocial than a Melancholic. His talents are often in music, art, science, or the thinking fields. Such children should be started in sporting events early, when they may find it less objectionable.

If you've waited too long or they just are not interested, don't push them! It is important that you accept the cerebral loner or music lover for what he is. The world has benefited much from musicians and artists who had no interest whatsoever in athletics. But even so, learning to hit a softball, play volleyball, and swim reasonably well should be encouraged to enrich his church youth camp experiences and for his own physical well-being.

Melancholic young people are often uncoordinated and find sports difficult. Since they take failure much more seriously than do the other temperaments, they tend to withdraw rather than be publicly humiliated. Don't be deceived by their assertion "I don't like sports" or "I can't do it." Many such children have benefited by loving parents who gave them enough backyard practice until they could play reasonably well.

Sports Aren't Everything!

You may think we are putting too much emphasis on participation in sports, since some young people are just not well-coordinated but can do other things easily. If that is true for your child, accept him as he is, find his area of talent, and help him to excel at it. But don't make the mistake of many parents, who let the child's first feeble attempts at sports discourage him so much that he quits. With encouragement he can find some sport that he can handle well. This will help him adjust to others his age and build his self-confidence.

Even more important, athletics are an excellent training ground for life. They require learning, practice, self-discipline, sacrifice, and an ability to get along with other people. It has been my observation that by watching an athlete perform, you will find out what kind of person he is, for the pressure of competition reveals the participant's spirit. What he is on the playing field, he will be in life. If a child is selfish and unfair, it will surface on the playing field. If he is a griper or a quitter, sports will bring it out into the open so you can work on it.

We had a Sanguine-Melancholic friend who was not well-coordinated and whose father, although a superb athlete himself, had neglected to train his son to be any kind of a sportsman. Whenever he engaged in a sport he compensated for his lack of playing ability by cheating. When my husband used to come home from golfing with this man, he would grumble, "His best club was his pencil. He never adds all his strokes." Years later his tendency to cheat at golf spread to cheating in other areas more serious, and it cost him dearly.

Parents of Melancholic children are often disappointed to find that their son or daughter withdraws from others and enjoys isolating himself in his room to study, paint, listen to music, or work on some science project. The more gifted he is, the more likely he will be to resort to such hermitlike behavior. It is so important that you use discretion with such a child! A sports-loving father (particularly a Choleric, but also some Sanguines) usually does everything wrong when this child resists athletics and withdraws from his peers. He may shame, ridicule, or coerce him, only to find he is driving him deeper into the cave of solitude. Once you have tried to bring him out, accept him for who and what he is. Then he can pursue his projects with your blessing and develop his native creativity and talents.

Young People and Their Church

Parents who take an active part in a Bible-believing church have a great advantage over an unchurched family in raising teens. This doesn't mean that the teen who goes to church is immune to worldly temptations, since many public schools have turned into zoos today. Drugs, sexual immorality, pornography, violence, and witchcraft have replaced what was once a great educational system.

Unless children are sent to a Christian school, which I advise wherever possible, or they are home-schooled, their public school is likely to present very different morals from what they get at church or at home. The church should become an ideal haven that reinforces what the home supports. At the Christian youth group they can be taught godly principles for living and can enjoy a social life that reflects the standards of the home.

Most progressive churches have a youth pastor (or dedicated couple) who plans an attractive junior high and high school program that appeals to the average Christian teenager. Yet at some time during these years, don't be surprised if your son or daughter becomes disenchanted with his youth group. Often parents blindly take the side of their teen when personality conflicts or personal jealousies flare up. To let them drop out of youth activities for such reasons can sometimes prove fatal! With our four young people it seemed we usually had one who was displeased with his Sunday school class or youth group, but we insisted that he attend anyway, and we frequently found that before the year was out he had changed his mind.

Christian parents should be supportive of their local church in front of their teens and should insist on their active participation in everything their church offers for their age level. Don't be surprised if they announce, "I'm not going to that church or youth group anymore!" You are the parent and they are the children and your authority has now been challenged. If you tolerate this rebellion, non-Christian friends will take the place of their church friends and then you will have a greater potential for problems.

Your church and its youth program are not perfect (don't expect them to be), but they are so much better than the alternatives that the question of whether they attend should not even be an option open to them. If the youth group is not acceptable, then you should find a church that offers a ministry to teens that is acceptable. We found that the keys to the family car were all that it took to keep even our twelfth-graders consistent when they didn't want to be. Young people, like children, will test your rules. Don't let their test catch you by surprise. Expect it and be ready with an answer.

Offer Yourself

What if your teenager's youth group is not all that it should be? We have found that the problem is usually the lack of high-quality adult leadership. All Christian parents want a good youth program but few are willing to offer themselves to God to provide the leadership such a program requires. Years ago our youth pastor went against common practice and started challenging parents to work in the group where their teens attended. He wisely felt they had a natural interest in that group and should be most willing to sacrifice their time to make the youth program a success.

At first the teens complained, "We can't get away from our parents!" And some parents were afraid it would alienate them from their teens. But actually quite often the opposite happened: The young people and their parents had many interests in common and enjoyed doing things together, and most of the kids became quite proud of the fact that their parents were leaders or helpers.

As we look back on the years with our young people, we treasure the church-sponsored outings, beach parties, river trips, camps, evangelistic outreaches, and other events we shared together. And we praise God for the vital contribution the church has made in each of their lives. One Sunday a nervous mother shook hands with my husband at the church door after the service and said, "Pastor, please pray for our family. We have three teenagers all at the same time." On the way home he described her problem to me. "That woman is having all kinds of trouble with her teens, and the only spiritual help they get is from attending Sunday school and church when they feel like it. They never come to the youth activities planned for them on weekends or the Wednesday Youth Bible study."

We had three teens at the same time, seventh through twelfth grades, and everything was not always perfect, but we loved it. One big difference was that our young people participated actively in all the youth activities, and most of the time willingly. We praise God for the ministry that the church and its youth groups have had on the lives of our young people, as do many other parents who insisted that their children participate. In many cases, those who refused to encourage and occasionally force their young people to attend have lived to regret it because their teenagers took up with friends who were involved in activities that led them away from the Lord.

Screening Teenage Friendships

Peer pressure is so powerful in the lives of teenagers that at some stages in their development their friends have a greater influence on them than parents do. Between age

15 and their senior year of high school (depending on their temperament), the influence of these friends can undo much of the good that parents have trained into their children. On the other hand, friends who are active Christian young people will fortify good family instructions and standards.

First Corinthians 15:33 contains an important instruction that surprises many parents. God says, "Do not be deceived: Bad company corrupts good morals" (NASB). We have seen unwise parents stand by and pray that their young people would discontinue a deep friendship with those of their own sex or the "steady" of the opposite sex that was having a bad influence on them. In reality, they were being derelict in their parental duties by not refusing to let them run around with those unsaved friends. As long as your children live in your home and eat your meals, you have the right to guide them into the proper friendships.

The problem is, as even Dr. Benjamin Spock now admits, that too many parents are afraid of their teenagers' disapproval or fear the words "I hate you!" It may surprise you that many teens in a fit of rage have said that to their parents, but it is a temporary feeling caused because they can't have their own way, particularly with friends of their choosing.

At a time of teenagers' spiritual carnality, you will find that the young people outside the church have much more of an attraction to them than the kids in church. The problem is not that the Christian kids are a "drag," but that the worldly ways of your teenager's friends are more appealing to him because he himself isn't right spiritually. If you let him drop out of the youth group at church and run with the world, they will eventually corrupt him.

A Crucial Turning Point

My husband is in the ministry today because when he turned 17 his widowed mother found 1 Corinthians 15:33 in her devotions and realized that his boyhood friends were turning him away from the Lord. She sat him down one Saturday morning and said, " Those boys are having a bad influence on your life, and I want you to break off with them and find your friends at church."

Naturally, he refused! What carnal, self-willed teenager wouldn't? She then said, "Young man, you are too big for me to spank anymore, but I can't stand by and have your carnal life influencing your younger brother and sister." Then through her tears she added, "As long as you park your feet under my table, you will do what I say; otherwise you will have to find another place to live."

He was furious for weeks, but finally he grudgingly obeyed. Today he claims that time as the turning point in his life. Personally, I thank God he had a mother like that!

Christian young people can help each other. All teens need someone in whom they can confide, particularly when they have a conflict with their parents. It is far better that they have a Christian friend who shares their spiritual convictions and who comes from a home where they have similar standards. Unsaved young people at a time like that will only feed their rebellion.

Remember the biblical principle: "A natural man does not accept the things of the Spirit of God; for they are foolishness to him, and he cannot understand them because they are spiritually appraised" (1 Corinthians 2:14 NASB).

17

Dating and Careers

Probably the greatest fears that a parent has today when his or her young person begins to date are the threat of a sexual encounter with the opposite sex, teenage pregnancy, and drugs. However, dating can be an exciting experience not only for the teenager but for the father and mother as well. Some parents say it is traumatic, while others find it an enjoyable part of raising their children. Either way, you can expect your young people to date or wish they could. As early as junior high, peer pressure for dating is a strong influence, particularly on girls.

The main cause for emotional trauma during the dating stage of life is that it usually catches both the teenager and his parents unprepared. The young people have no idea what their parents expect of them, and the parents are not always in agreement with each other. That's a formula for disaster! We prepare our children for Sunday school, regular school, birthdays, Christmas, swimming lessons, and almost every other event in life. Why not prepare them for dating? We found that if the first child is properly prepared, it is a relatively simple matter to get younger brothers and sisters to accept the same standards. If parents strike out with the first, they may also lose with the others.

Dating causes fear in many parents' heart for several reasons. First, it is a giant step toward independence. Parents are allowing their young person to go out the door without adult supervision with another teen who is also experiencing a newfound independence. They lose a large degree of control over their teenager when he goes out with someone else for two to four hours at a time. Second, some parents haven't learned to trust their children. Dating accentuates that lack of trust. Third, they have not prepared guidelines in advance, so the independence of dating exaggerates their fears.

Guidelines for Dating

We have had the privilege of using our guidelines for dating on ten children, four of our own plus six missionary children whose parents sent them to live with us for their junior and senior years of high school. Whenever we accepted teenagers of missionaries, it was with the proviso that they agreed to our dating guidelines. Although there were confrontations at times, both with the missionaries' young people and with our own, it was basically a very pleasurable experience. The guidelines were explained in advance and everyone seemed to understand what was expected of him or her. Here are the standards we have developed through the years.

1. *Dating is for 15-year-olds and over.* Reserving dating for 15-year-olds is no problem for boys. In fact, many of them are not interested until much later (or couldn't afford it even if they were). Girls are another matter! As we have seen, girls mature faster than boys both physically and socially, so they are often anxious to start dating very early. Unfortunately, the boys their own age are often disinterested, do not have driver's licenses, or do not appeal to the girls, so it is older boys who select the younger girls, and that presents its own problems. Although 15 is a recommended age to begin dating (depending on the maturity of the young person), this should not eliminate young people from enjoying each other's company at church youth group activities, camp, or the like. But official dating, when a boy comes to a girl's home to take her on a specified outing, should be reserved until after the fifteenth birthday.

2. *Date only Christians!* One cardinal principle that is clearly specified in the Word of God is "Do not be unequally yoked together with unbelievers" (2 Corinthians 6:14). Dating is a yoke of fellowship that can someday be a prelude to marriage. The way to help your young people avoid the emotional trauma of ever having to decide "Should I marry this unsaved person with whom I am very much in love or should we break up?" is to set a standard at the very beginning before any emotions get involved. It is very doubtful that your son or daughter will ever get seriously involved with anyone they do not date. This standard may cause a few tears when they are forbidden to keep company with the handsome high school quarterback with whom they are infatuated, but it could eliminate a major trauma later.

Through the years we have watched fine, dedicated Christians who dearly loved their children lose them because they did not set this standard. I mention this here because we have recently had to pray and cry with several of them who lived to regret it. We know of two such girls who were married at 18 and divorced at 19. Needless to say, both the parents and their girls were brokenhearted.

3. *Schedule a predating interview with the father.* This really sorts out the kind of guys that want to date your daughter. When a young man dates your daughter, it is serious business because he is going out with one of your most treasured possessions. If a person borrowed your car or boat, you would clearly set some guidelines for its use. It is even more important when a young man goes out with your daughter. This may scare some prospects away, but you will find that is the group you want your daughter to avoid anyway. Any boy who lacks the courage to look a girl's father in the eye when asking permission has no business dating her anyway.

This interview gives the father the opportunity to do four things: One, to see for himself that the young man is really a Christian (hearsay testimonies aren't always valid). Two, to check his vision for his own future. Does he have goals or plans for his life suitable for his age level? Do you detect a sense of responsibility and self-discipline in the young man? Is dating your daughter and getting her alone his only objective for the moment? Three, to clearly lay down the guidelines they are to follow. Don't expect your daughter to do this. It is embarrassing for her. Besides, something might be missed in the transmission.

Four, to size up the home life from which the lad comes. The answer to this question may not necessarily determine whether they can or cannot date, but if the young man loves and respects his parents, it helps you to know what to expect in your relationships with him. The converse is also true.

When your son wants to date a Christian girl, it is somewhat easier for you to share with him your guidelines, which are essentially the same as those for girls. He then sets the standards with the girl he goes out with. If he dates the same girl two or three times and you don't know her personally, you would be wise to have him bring her along to a "Four F" outing or set up a casual meeting with both you and your spouse. (The reason I suggest that the mother be in on this interview or get-together is because it may be easy for a cute girl to "bamboozle" the father. It takes a woman to evaluate a woman, particularly where her son is involved.)

Bill Gothard did us and thousands of other parents a great favor in teaching at his seminars that guidelines for dating, including an interview with the father, were very important. It really fortified our procedure and in recent years has made the process much easier for many Christian young people to accept.

4. *All dates must be approved in advance.* Until young people get acquainted with you and your guidelines, don't let them stampede you into a quick approval of some type of activity which you do not favor. We made it clear to our teens that approved dating could include all church activities and outings, chaperoned parties, sports events, and special events they wished to request. The "don't bother to

ask" list included movies, dances, unchaperoned private parties, or any activity where drinking or drugs took place. We included movies and dances in this list for several obvious reasons. Most movies have some sexual overtones, even the PG-13 movies, and in many there are even brief scenes of nudity. Dancing and drugs are often combined at the same social events, so we just eliminated any chances of our young people being thrown into these temptations or embarrassing situations.

5. *Until high school graduation, double-dating only.* Probably the one standard the kids objected to most was double-dating with another Christian couple. There is safety in numbers—not totally, but some. The main reason for this, however, is to force them to make plans in advance and to avoid long periods of time when they can drift into "heavy couple talk." Under a wave of libido and the romance of the moment, it is easy to make premature love statements and engage in physical touching that could easily lead the couple to sexual intercourse. The presence of another couple cuts down on this possibility drastically, even though it doesn't eliminate it entirely.

It is sometimes admittedly difficult to get up a double date, so to compensate for our stringent rules we bent over backward to make the family car available to our son whenever it was legitimate. Usually if your son has the wheels, it isn't too hard for him to find a friend to double-date with him—that is, if he really wants to.

6. *Absolutely no parking!* Every city has an area where young people like to gather and park their cars. Some may be great places to park and "look over the lights of the

city," but it is not too good an environment for avoiding youthful temptations. At this stage of life, touching the opposite sex is exciting, stimulating, and dangerous. We believe dating is for fun and social fellowship, not to tempt their self-control.

One of our children testily said, "Dad, I get the feeling you don't trust us!" to which he replied, "You're right. I don't trust you, myself, or anyone else when they make provision for the flesh." You may ask, "Didn't your children ever park during their dating years?" We aren't so naive as to think they didn't, but if they did, we wanted it clearly understood that it was against our rules. As one girl said, "Whenever I was tempted to park while on a date with a boy, I was always afraid my father might rise up out of the backseat."

7. *No undue public show of affection.* Love is beautiful to both teens and adults, but public demonstrations of affection that border on suggestiveness is harmful to the individual's testimony and may imply moral license to others. The Bible teaches us to "avoid the very appearance of evil." The Christian community applauds teenagers who obviously love each other but have enough self-respect not to maul each other in public. Proper dating should not detract from a young person's testimony or spiritual growth; besides, open expressions of affection today may prove embarrassing later when the interest in that person is gone.

8. *Curfew at 11:00 P.M. for girls and 11:30 P.M. for boys* (with approved exceptions). Except for certain well-chaperoned functions that we knew in advance would last later than 10:30 P.M., we expected our girls home at 11:00

and our boys at 11:30. (It took about half an hour to escort two girls and another fellow home before meeting his curfew.) These early deadlines were universally resisted at first and were probably earlier than those set by most parents. But our reasoning was that there is very little wholesome activity going on in our city after 11:00 P.M. The good coffee shops close then, and we think teenagers should be home by that time.

Admittedly most parents are more lenient. One of our daughters tearfully wailed, "Dad, I'm the only girl in the church that has to be in by 11:00." He lovingly reassured her, "I can't help it if the rest of the parents are wrong." Our son said after marriage, "One thing I found embarrassing about our family's dating rules was that all the girls I dated had a later curfew than I did." One girl asked him, "Why are you bringing me home at 11:00? I don't have to be in until 12:00." In spite of the embarrassment and some problems, now that they are raised, we have no regrets. In fact, our daughter, who often chafed under the curfew, commented four months after the birth of her daughter, "Remember those dating rules? We're planning to use the same ones for our little girl when she's old enough to date!" (Life looks different when you're the parent.)

A problem for some parents may be how to enforce the curfew. Whatever hour you set for curfew will usually be considered too early and may be ignored. This creates much unnecessary conflict between parents and teens. We solved that problem very simply by clearly pointing out that every minute they were late coming home would cost them 15 minutes shorter time on the next date. One young man brought our daughter home so late on a date that their next one was only 1 1/2 hours long. Young people need to know that you keep your word, so they will probably test your rules. Be sure you don't flunk their test!

Some parents may think our guidelines are too rigid and not "socially correct" for this generation. My response to that is I would rather fall on the side of being too careful than not being cautious enough with my children. We have only one chance to raise them. There are no second chances. With the increase in teenage pregnancies, drug use, and alcoholism, I encourage parents to be strong in their guidelines. It could literally mean the difference between life and death.

Too often parents think, "I can trust my children," so they let them make their own dating standards or give them too much flexibility. Admittedly, in some cases this has worked very well, but in many others we have seen the good training of early childhood and adolescent years tragically marred by too much freedom in the teen years. Such parents have forgotten the powerful influence that teenagers have on each other and the tidal waves of libido that strike all normal young people. It is tragic when the self-control lessons of childhood are overpowered by these new and exciting drives that come at a time when teenagers are least able to cope with them.

In all of life these are the years of greatest emotional instability. It is so easy to make decisions on the basis of emotion rather than mind and will. Someone has said, "When the emotion and will are in conflict, the emotions invariably win." This is dangerous because emotionally made decisions are almost always wrong. It takes a good deal of maturity for any person to learn that only when the mind and emotions agree is it right to proceed with anything.

And even then the mind should be guided by the Word of God. Solomon said, "A wise son makes a glad father, but a foolish son is the grief of his mother" (Proverbs 10:1). That is also true of a daughter.

You may not agree with the rules laid down by the parents of the young person your son or daughter dates, but if you can't respect their right to establish them, you had better urge your teen to date someone else. We were extremely fortunate with our eldest daughter in that the parents of the young man she was dating, who is today her husband, encouraged him not to object to our rules. Instead, they convinced him he had to respect our right to make them. When those two were married, the event also united two families. Now this couple has been used of God in ministering to thousands of high school young people and they have provided a good example of how Christian young people should face these tempestuous years.

Too Much Too Late

At our seminars many parents of teenagers ask us, "How do you establish these rules when your young people are already dating on their own terms?" The answer we give is, "Very gradually!" But be sure you do it. Prayerfully decide what rules you are going to establish, then sit down and very humbly admit to your son or daughter that you have been careless in your parental responsibility and that you love them and care about their future so you're going to establish some new guidelines for dating. Don't be surprised at the explosive reaction you get, but when the dust clears, you will have established a program that will guide your teenager in making some of the greatest decisions of his life.

When we planned a second Family Life Seminar in Houston, Texas, a man volunteered for the job of chairman. He is a successful businessman in that city and very active in his church. When asked why he was so enthusiastic about our returning there, he told us that he had attended our first seminar at a time when the oldest of his five sons was dating pretty much on any terms he chose. After hearing our guidelines, he went home and established a similar procedure. Although difficult at first, the decision had so changed his son and consequently the atmosphere of their home life that he wanted other families in Houston to share the same opportunity for blessing.

Graduation Warning

A warning to parents about graduation parties may seem out of line here, but unfortunately there have been too many graduation tragedies that could have been avoided with proper parental oversight. All too often alcohol, drugs, sex, and wild celebrations have scarred the lives of far too many graduates, and in some cases have ended their lives. Parents, be alert and help your child make wise decisions. Because they are graduates, they feel like throwing caution to the wind and "living it up"—only to regret it later on.

After Graduation

The last big stage of teen training is in the post-high-school years. It is during this time that your teens will be forced to make some of the greatest decisions of their life.

Should they go to college or learn a skill? Where should they go to school or work? The answers to these questions will ultimately have a bearing on such decisions as what their life's vocation will be, who they will marry, where they will work and live, and where they will go to church.

These are momentous decisions which will chart the course of their whole life. Happy is the teenager whose relationship to his parents is such that they can serve as his counselors in making these decisions. The wise man of Proverbs said, "Without consultation, plans are frustrated, but with many counselors they succeed" (Proverbs 15:22 NASB). No one has the graduate's best interest at heart like his parents. So who is better qualified to be his counselors? But at this stage he may receive it reluctantly or may not receive it at all. If you have not built the parent-counselor relationship between you and your child by graduation, it is very difficult to establish it in time for these vital years. But at least you can offer your suggestions.

Generally speaking (and that is always a dangerous term), the Christian community has urged its young people to go to college as a means of increasing a young person's potential of service for the Lord. But the romance of "college after high school" that has dominated the post-World-War-II years is coming to an end. Vocationally, there are many better-paying jobs open to young people that provide a very constructive and challenging career. At one time a college education was required to get the best jobs, depending on a person's temperament and aptitudes. But today that is not necessarily true. However, academic training will give a young person more versatility for possible future careers, including Christian service, plus the experience that builds self-discipline in his life.

One of the dangers of a secular college education today is that the whole educational system has been taken over by an atheistic, humanistic philosophy that is largely anti-God, anti-moral, and anti-American. Such a system has a radical influence on the majority of students, even those who come from Christian homes.

From my viewpoint as a Christian parent, and as the registrar for Christian Heritage College for over five years, I am convinced that all Christian young people should avoid secular college as long as possible and trust God to provide them with a Christian college experience.

There are excellent Christian colleges and universities with full accreditation that offer a good academic education. In a Christian setting your young people can best be trained to be the spiritual leaders of tomorrow, no matter what their ultimate vocation happens to be. Such schools give them an ideal environment in which to evaluate their vocational potential, to seek God's will for their lives, and to make friends with other Christians who are faced with the same decisions at this stage in life. Christian college professors will influence the young people spiritually, whereas secular college professors often do just the opposite.

The Christian environment also surrounds young people with worthy companions while they are in the zenith of their emotionally combustible years. During the college years many young people meet their future marriage partner, and where better than in a Christian environment to meet such a person? (Those students who plan to go into medicine, law, science, or other fields that may require study at a secular college should consider one or two years first at a Christian college or Bible school to prepare them for the anti-Christian philosophy and environment they will ultimately encounter.)

The city in which we ministered for over 20 years had seven secular colleges and universities. We have seen scores of fine Christian young people fall apart spiritually and even turn their back on biblical teaching while attending such colleges. Many have married unsaved college friends and have missed God's best for their lives. We have heard Christian parents say, "We can't afford to send our young people to a Christian college. We will send them to a state school; it is much cheaper!" It actually turns out to be the most expensive thing they ever did.

In many cases, the parents couldn't afford *not* to send their children to a Christian college.

The Real Purpose for Children

The real purpose for Christians having children is to bring them to adulthood to serve and glorify the Lord. To do so, they must study the Bible to become "approved unto God, a worker who does not need to be ashamed, rightly dividing the word of truth" (2 Timothy 2:15). This doesn't mean that God wants all young people to be missionaries or ministers, but it does mean they can be trained to be Christian professionals in any field they enter.

One of our dearest friends is a plastering contractor who had three years of Bible school training before he became an apprentice plasterer. During the past 30 years he has held every office in the church, taught a Sunday school class, and led many people to Christ. This man and his parents feel that those three years in Bible school were a mighty good investment!

The teen years are so important. You as parents can now look at the results of your years of service in raising your children. I pray that you can say these children were a gift from God and that you were privileged to have a part in their upbringing.

18

What Rights Do Children Have?

Parents hear a lot of discussion about the rights of their children these days and may even become intimidated into believing that perhaps they are restricting their children from the proper rights they deserve. What are their rights?

Children's rights advocates will tell you that children have "rights" that allow them to make their own choices in how they act and what they do. And the same group of "children's rights" advocates believe that it takes the government and its programs to raise a child. Hillary Rodham Clinton's book, *It Takes a Village*, is really promoting the idea that it takes a village, a community, a government to raise our children. The book is a direct promotional for the Clinton Administration's socialistic programs that want to change the way children are raised and who is responsible for raising them. But we must remember that

Scripture repeatedly puts the control of raising children in the hands of the mother and father.

That is one of the purposes in writing this book. One purpose is to help you understand your child's temperament better so you can properly train him, but the other is to remind you who the children belong to and who is responsible for their upbringing.

Children Do Have Rights

Every child who is brought into this world has the right to expect the following provisions.

1) A child has the right to have parents who are committed to providing for his needs. 2) A child has the right to have parents who will love and nurture him toward adulthood. 3) A child has the right to be told no at the appropriate times in his life. 4) A child has the right to be protected from some of the dangers that would destroy him and how he can say no to these dangers. 5) A child has the right to be taught that there are significant differences between boys and girls. 6) A child has the right to know that obedience to his parents and authorities is expected of him and is best for him. 7) A child has the right to a proper education that does not conflict with the morals and values of his parents' teachings, even if the parent has to become the educator. 8) A child has the right to be exposed to biblical truth that will enable him to discern right from wrong. 9) Finally, a child has the right to be introduced to the love of the Lord so he can receive Him at an early age. There are many more things that could be added to this list, but the above rights are the

most basic ones that benefit a child and provide a bright hope for this future.

Warning to Parents

You have about 18 years to accomplish what you desire to teach and build into your child. During that time your child will spend 12 years or more under the supervision of an educator. Guard that time, for you cannot repeat it. Make sure that you carefully choose who will be privileged to mold your child's thinking and direct his values during this very impressionable stage of his life.

The goals and agenda of the educational system, the accuracy and bias of the curriculum used, the qualifications and character of the teacher, and the peer environment will all have an influence in molding your child's thinking and direction. For this reason many parents have chosen to put their children in private Christian schools, and many others have decided to teach them at home in a home-schooling program. Whatever you choose, do it prayerfully, seeking God's help, because choices made during this part of your child's life will almost certainly affect the direction of his life.

In addition to providing for the academic education of your child, it is very important for you to remember that he has the right to spiritual development as well. This starts with a good home that puts an emphasis on loving and obeying God. Parents who live what they teach to their children will make a great personal impression on their lives. But they also need the support of a good Bible-teaching church and youth group. The weekly sermons and Bible lessons right out of God's Word will help to undergird what the parents try to live at home. Your children will then be able to develop friendships and have a social life that is more protected from the effects of the ungodly world outside.

Mission Possible!

It is not impossible to raise godly children today, but it is more difficult than previously, and parents need to take advantage of every opportunity possible to reinforce biblical principles in their minds. That is why we have provided the entire following chapter: to inspire you to follow the responsibility God has given you.

Start when your children are just beginning and understand what blends of temperaments they are, including the weaknesses you need to be watchful for, and then work to correct these weaknesses. Then make sure the educational program you choose for them reinforces your values. Next, be actively involved in a good church. Finally, spend much time in prayer for each child. Prayer does change things!

19

Is Good Training Really Possible?

It has been several years since the birth of any of my grandchildren, and many years since my own children were born. Methods of delivery and hospitalization have changed dramatically, but one basic part of childbirth does not change. That is the immediate feeling that comes over a new parent of the awesome responsibility that lies ahead of her or him. Can I do it properly? What does training really involve? Where do I go for help?

We parents of the present new generation used to carry our babies in one arm and Dr. Spock's book in the other. Unfortunately, he was not always right. Even he has admitted as much many years later. Today there are child-rearing books of all sorts—secular and spiritual, tolerant and rigid, passive and aggressive. You can pick any kind of helps you want, but I believe one of the best sources on training a child is from the words of the Creator Himself.

One of the most familiar verses from God's Word is Proverbs 22:6: "Train up a child in the way he should go, and when he is old he will not depart from it." I don't think God was referring to just disciplining a child. Discipline is an important part of good training, but by itself it does not bring about proper behavior. Then what does?

When Proverbs talks about training, it is the parents who are instructed to train their children. Let's examine the verse carefully.

1. *"Train up."* The Hebrew word for this relates to the inside of the mouth—the gums, the palate, or the roof of the mouth—and refers to the use of a bit or bridle that is placed in the mouth of an untamed horse. This is used to bring a wild horse into submission. Interesting visualization, isn't it?

James 3:3 gives further explanation of the use of the bit: "We put bits in horses' mouths that they may obey us, and we turn their whole body." The same bit that is used to tame a wild and self-willed horse is also used to guide the steps of a gentle and obedient horse. Scripture uses this clear illustration to teach us that all children need guidance and boundaries, and that one of the most important places to start is with the mouth. What you permit to come forth from a child's mouth very clearly demonstrates what is going on in his heart. You cannot successfully "train up" a child until he has learned about submitting his will, and often his will is revealed by his mouth.

In other words, it is necessary to bring a child's mouth into submission in order to teach him to obey his parents, and thus turn him in the direction that is right for him to go. Children who do not learn to willingly obey when they are young will rarely accept guidance from their parents later on. They need to turn from their own selfish ways so that one day they will obediently follow the teachings of Jesus Christ.

2. *"A child."* The same Hebrew word that is used here for "child" is found several other places in the Bible. Here are a few examples:

- First Samuel 4:21 refers to a young infant that has just been born.
- Genesis 21:14 uses this word when it refers to Ishmael, who was 15 years old.
- Genesis 37:30 makes reference to the child Joseph at 17 years of age.
- Genesis 34:5 refers to Jacob's daughter, who was the age to be married.

The time span for "a child" can be from infancy until the age when he leaves home to marry and establish his own home.

3. *"In the way he should go."* This phrase more literally means "in keeping with his way" or "in accordance with the way he was designed by God." This does not mean the way the *parents* think he should go, but simply the way he was designed by God—in other words, his temperament, which is God's design. God's design never contradicts His Word. This is not a choice on moral behavior but on the gifts and talents that God gives to each child.

Within the framework of the principles of God, train your child according to his temperament or in keeping with the characteristics and talents he has been given. You should not train a Sanguine the same as a Phlegmatic or a Choleric the same as a Melancholic. Each child needs to be trained according to the original way God designed for him.

4. *"And when he is old."* The word "old" here does not mean 60 or 70 years old. It refers to a male child when he begins to grow hair on his face or when he begins to enter the age of maturity.

5. *"He will not depart from it."* He will always be the temperament God has given him, and your training will not have been in vain. You will have helped him enrich and improve the weaknesses of his natural God-given talents.

Not Perfect But Diligent

God does not demand perfect parents, but He has laid down a few basic requirements for training our children. We can fall short in many areas, but God does expect us to train our children in obedience and to bring them into subjection. Teaching obedience is more than giving instructions. It is instructing and then insisting on the child's compliance. Too often we tell the child what we want him to do, but we neglect to insist that he do it.

A terrific missionary, after 20 years of service, was passed over for leadership because he repeatedly refused to carry out orders the way he had been instructed. After years of effective service as an assistant, and even though the heads of the organization loved and admired him and were fully aware of his great contribution to the work of the Lord, they could not trust him with complete control because he consistently refused to carefully follow instructions. He did not fight or argue but simply did things his own way. Somewhere, as a child, absolute obedience was not insisted upon and, consequently, he missed a great opportunity in life and had to go through an unnecessary and traumatic experience.

Effective training can be condensed down to a simple formula:

Instruction + Love + Insistence = Effective Training

Each step is an important ingredient in training, and none can be omitted if we are to enjoy the desired results. When instruction is given and followed by insistence to obey, it may well result in rebellion if love has been left out. Instruction and love are of little value when there is no insistence to comply to the instructions.

There is really no such thing as the "perfect" parent. And even if perfection could be reached, our children would not always be happy. Their basic temperaments have a lot to do with their natural happiness. You cannot judge the effectiveness of your training by the happiness of your children. Even with all your dedicated efforts to fill your children's lives with pleasure, each one will still experience many moments of real emotional pain that are necessary for growing up. Too often we are led to believe that we carry full responsibility for every phase of our children's emotional well-being. An unhappy child causes his parents to feel guilty and to blame themselves. As each child goes through growth changes, there will be peaks of joy and depths of sadness, though neither can be counted on to last.

The most important challenge of being a parent is not to be perfect, but to teach the child to one day take full responsibility for his own life. The child enters the world totally helpless, so helpless that he cannot even scratch where he itches. And we as parents are to take that helpless infant to the place of complete responsibility during the course of 18 to 20 years. In order to meet that goal, it is necessary that the child experience for himself some of the emotional pains that are true to life so that he can grow into an authentic adult.

God Keeps His Promises

I don't claim to know and understand everything about God (though I'm working on that each day), but I do know that He keeps His promises and that I can trust Him to do what He says He will do. When your children are acting rebellious and living contrary to the standards you have set for them, and your heart seems like it is breaking in two, it is easy to cry out to God and ask where He is and why He isn't keeping His Word.

This is when you need to spend much time in prayer, perhaps even on your knees, with the Bible readily available to minister to you and to help you focus on things above, rather than on the dreadful circumstances you are in. Commit your children into His care and His loving but tough discipline. There is hardly a Christian parent anywhere who has not had to turn a child over to God's discipline somewhere along the way. God has His own ways of dealing with rebellious children to bring them back to the truth.

I recall one beautiful family of four. The mother and father were very loving and exemplified patience, gentleness, and kindness to each other; most people would classify them as an ideal family. Rarely a Sunday went by when they were not in church with their two children. But there was one critical area that was omitted from their home, and it turned out to be a tragic mistake. The biblical principle that the father and mother were placed in authority over the children was never practiced in this home. These fine people never insisted that their two children obey them. They let the children make most of their own choices regarding their friends, their activities, and the hours they kept. When the parents did not approve they never made an issue of conflict over it.

Eventually the day came when the children followed their own desires instead of the wishes and convictions of their parents. Both of these young people lived carnal lives as they left home, and eventually both married unbelievers. After many heartbreaking disappointments, both ended up with very stormy divorces. It seemed like the bottom fell out of everything they touched, and when young people hit bottom, often the only place left to go is back home to Mom and Dad.

Today they are struggling to get their lives back together again. But it didn't have to be like this. How much better when parents bring their children to the place of submission and obedience and the children follow Ephesians 6:1: "Children, obey your parents in the Lord, for this is right."

Too Late to Change?

What should parents do when they realize they have been negligent but their children are now half-grown toward adulthood? Because nothing is impossible with God, you can still move forward and make changes. Consider the following steps, regardless of what stage your children are in, and trust God to bring about change in all of your lives.

1. Recognize and admit the areas of your failure. Ask God to show you where you are weak and be willing to name the problems: pride, irritability, permissiveness, inconsistency, wrong priorities, lack of spiritual leadership, poor role model for your children, etc.

2. Confess your failures before God and ask for His forgiveness. First John 1:9 says, "If we confess our sins, He is faithful and just to forgive us our sins and to cleanse us from all unrighteousness."

3. Prayerfully and lovingly confess your failures to the family members you have offended, and pray that they will be forgiving. First Peter 4:8 says, "Above all things have fervent love for one another, for love will cover a multitude of sins."

4. Ask God to help you change your habits and develop a new plan to correct the old. The Bible has many helps for laying out a new way to live using godly principles.

5. Trust God to change your life and to correct the bad habits that have developed in your children.

6. Begin living from this new point in your spiritual life and not under the guilt of the past, for it has been forgiven.

7. Now expect God to do great things in your life and in your family.

Wait for God to Work

Keep in mind that your heavenly Father loves you and your children and is more desirous than you are that you be a successful parent and that your children obey His commands. But you do have to follow His principles. Now be patient while He does a work in you that will influence your whole family.

Don't be impatient for God to bring about change! You be faithful to what you have promised to do; love your children just as they are and wait patiently for God to work in their lives.

20

Teaching Right and Wrong

Parenting would be a lot simpler if children came already equipped with a knowledge of right and wrong. Then all that parents would have to do is encourage and keep them on the right path during those 18 or so years. But that's not the way it is. God intended the mother and father to spend time and effort training their children in the way they should go.

Dr. Lawrence Kohlberg, Professor of Education and Social Psychology at Harvard University, says that children up to the age of ten are rarely capable of making what most adults regard as "pure" moral judgments. Until at least that age, a child's notions of morality come not from any strong sense of right and wrong but from his feelings about what the consequences might be. He obeys rules to avoid being punished, or he is nice to other people so that others will be nice to him. It's a rather selfish outlook on life, but that's the way kids are.

Too often we react emotionally to the things our children do, not because of the behavior itself, but because of what we read into it. When a child takes a toy from the corner store, you could consider him destined to be a thief. When a little fellow strikes a smaller child, he could be thought of as a lifelong bully, or when he tells a lie, we may have a tendency to think of him as a committed liar.

As our fears take over, we judge ourselves and then berate ourselves for having failed as parents. But when we calmly try to understand our children with their different temperaments and what motives were behind their actions, we will be better able to help them understand right from wrong. They need to learn early that God does not approve of stealing, lying, or hitting other people. But don't panic when your child follows his sin nature. Use that experience to teach him that he has sinned against God's standards for right and wrong and that sin needs to be confessed and corrected.

Teaching the Difference

There is great controversy over how you can effectively teach a child to discern right from wrong. There is the philosophy described in Hillary Clinton's book, *It Takes a Village,* that says children are essentially competent beings that simply need to be nurtured. Unfortunately, this view seems very unrealistic and out of touch with the vast majority of children in America today. Don't they ever need to be disciplined or corrected for wrong deeds?

On the other hand is the opposite philosophy, such as is described in former Vice President Dan Quayle's book,

The American Family, that supports control and punishment as "a way to shape behavior toward respect and obedience." There seems to be growing support for teaching children their proper place in the home and society, and applying appropriate punishment for disobedient acts.

I support Dan Quayle's idea for disciplining children because it more closely follows the biblical teachings. Proverbs 29:15 says, "The rod and reproof give wisdom, but a child left to himself brings shame to his mother." Far too many children in today's society have been left to themselves and have brought shame to their mothers and fathers. Regardless of what temperament your child may be, you need to have a plan ready for his discipline and punishment in order to impress upon his mind the difference between right and wrong. The stronger your child's will and stubbornness, such as a Choleric or Phlegmatic, the more intense the punishment needs to be. The more sensitive the child, like the Sanguine or melancholy, there may be less punishment needed. They can usually be directed by a stern look or a good reprimand.

Good morals need to be taught and practiced. A good time to teach and discuss morality is when a child has done something praiseworthy or is indecisive about a problem. It is beneficial to help a child come to decisions by reasoning out what is good and right. For example, Mary had promised to go over to Sally's house to spend the night. Sally had made great plans and was very elated over the upcoming event. However, another invitation was given to Mary to do something she liked even better and with friends she enjoyed even more. Now she had a tough decision to make.

Her parents granted her the right to decide but encouraged her to think about the moral issues in her choice. She was told she should do what she thought was right. Together they discussed who she had made a promise to. If that person trusted her to do what she said she would do, and if she breaks her promise and does something else, she would hurt her friend. After awhile she concluded that she would be too unhappy with herself if she broke her promise to her friend Sally.

Emphasize Fairness

I believe it is important to emphasize the concept of fairness. All morality boils down to the question of what is just and fair. God's standards for behavior are absolutely in line with this. Children develop a sensitivity of what is fair very early. Every parent has heard their child cry out, "That's just not fair!" (Sometimes they say this just to try to get their own way.)

Parents need to find different ways to teach values to their children that can be integrated into everyday activities, such as casual conversations around the dinner table, riding in the car, or anywhere the family spends time together. It can be as simple as asking everyone a question that needs to be answered, such as "What did you say or do this week that you think God was pleased about?"

Be careful that each child with their varying temperaments be included in giving an answer. One child may say that he had stuck up for a new kid on the playground when all the other kids were mean to him. Mother may say that she finished a project that she had been putting off for a long time. Father's good deed may be that he confronted a man in the office that continually used the Lord's name in vain. Another child may say that he had told a buddy how to receive Jesus into his heart.

The conversation that follows seeks to sort out the values in each of their replies—loyalty to a friend and courage to go against the group, persistence in pursuit of a goal and setting priorities of one's time, standing alone for one's spiritual convictions, and sharing with a friend a life-changing experience instead of keeping one's mouth shut.

Other questions may relate to how a person would handle certain circumstances or how they would help another person in a given problem. Not only do discussions like these pull values from each person, but they also help the children realize that you respect their viewpoints equally with the adults in your family. All family members should be treated with dignity when giving their ideas. It also gives you a chance to see how the different temperaments are thinking, so that you can direct their value system to keep in line with biblical truth.

Sassiness Not Accepted

One mother's advice to her married daughter when her first child was born was, "Don't take any sass!" Good sound advice, but it must be carried out by both parents. Sassiness shows disrespect to the one being addressed. It should not be allowed between siblings or to either parent. The Sanguine child will just be "quick on the lip" and then be sorry for it later on. The Choleric will indulge in sarcasm without being too quick to repent. A sassy child will not respect authority nor will he have a submissive spirit, but both are essential to obedience.

Parents go through an emotional shock with their first child's attempt to disregard the parent's authority. They bring that precious gift from God home from the hospital and that infant lies in his cradle looking like he has been carried to earth in the arms of angels. A beautiful picture to behold! Then shortly, some ten or twelve months later, that same angelic gift from God has the ability to curve his little rosebud lips and pronounce a distinct *no* in response to the parents' loving request. What a shock! It causes great concern when that little offspring stiffens his body and gives an emphatic *no* when he wants his own way.

This is just the beginning of a long road ahead of training that will determine the direction that little child will go. One day that little child will become a teenager, and what you have permitted him as a little child will certainly be carried on as he reaches his teens. When you begin by controlling his mouth, just as James 3:3 describes, you will begin to direct his entire body as well.

Society now has a generation of children that have been raised in a spirit of permissiveness who have been allowed to act disrespectfully to their parents and others in authority. Is it any wonder that we are reaping the consequences of a generation of unbridled tongues?

Choices Have Consequences

The young child who is permitted to raise his fist in defiance to his parents without correction will probably never be able to raise his face to Jesus Christ and say, "Dear Lord, what would You have me to do?" As James said, we need to put bits (controls) into the child's mouth so he will obey, and then we direct his whole body as well. The mouth reveals what is really in the heart. Matthew 15:18 says, "Those things which proceed out of the mouth come from the heart." The heart and the mouth are so closely related that it is necessary to control the mouth in order to reach the heart, which controls the direction the body goes.

This may be a partial explanation of the state of families today. Parents are allowing their children to make choices about how they speak to others and how they act. Choices do have consequences! And as the children grow they begin to reap some of the consequences of wrong choices.

Bob Vernon, former Assistant Chief of Police of the Los Angeles Police Department, says that by the year 2000, if conditions do not change, 50 percent of all babies born will be illegitimate. Can you imagine what the coming years will be like when half of all U.S. children will not know what it is like to have a mother and father in the home? Certainly illegitimacy will increase, crime will be greater than it is today, and the public schools will have difficulty trying to educate children who have little sense of right and wrong.

Bob Vernon went on to say that we need to get ready for an even greater anarchy of lawlessness by young people as an increasing crime wave sweeps America. Why? Because the vast majority of kids don't have a clue between right and wrong and have never had anyone put controls on their mouths and actions.

James 3:6 tells us the result of an unbridled tongue: "The tongue is a fire, a world of iniquity. The tongue is so set among our members that it defiles the whole body, and sets on fire the course of nature; and it is set on fire by hell." The next time you see a young person out of control, remember what James said about the power of the tongue and how it affects all the other members of our body. If a person's tongue is out of control, he will very likely have little respect for the law or for people in authority.

If you think this may be overstated, then I suggest that you visit a local public high school in your area and evaluate the situation for yourself. Talk to some of the dedicated long-term teachers and ask them if they have seen a difference in the youth of today compared to ten or fifteen years ago. Perhaps a visit such as this would shock parents of younger children into giving more attention to how they train their children right from wrong. It could help in determining what they need to focus on as society speeds their children along the road to destruction.

The Master Guidebook

Christian parents have a great responsibility in raising children and instilling into their young minds the truth about right and wrong. The good news is that Christian parents, or even Christian single parents, have the Master Guidebook, the Bible, to use in training their children. But this doesn't mean that your concerns are over, because kids from Christian homes still try to break the rules and often stretch their parents as far as they will stretch.

Children from good morally based homes may also try their hand at such things as lying, stealing, and using drugs or alcohol.

We live in a nation that no longer has a conscience, so parents must work harder at discerning the difference between right and wrong and also at being the protector, provider, educator, and example to their families.

21

A Biblical Guide for Discipline

My son, observe the commandment of your father,
And do not forsake the teaching of your mother;
Bind them continually on your heart;
Tie them around your neck.
When you walk about, they will guide you;
When you sleep, they will watch over you;
And when you awake, they will talk to you.
For the commandment is a lamp, and the teaching
   is light;
And reproofs for discipline are the way of life.

—Proverbs 6:20-23 NASB

Wise parents will study the book of Proverbs for inspiration and guidance on disciplining their children. It is important to know what God says about correction and reproof, but it is not enough to just know about it. You have to actually put it into practice before it will become effective in the life of your child. "Poverty and shame will come to him who neglects discipline, but he who regards reproof will be honored" (Proverbs 13:18 NASB).

Discipline is much more than punishment. Discipline is something you do *for* your child, not *to* your child. If parents have been consistent with their training, the chances are good that they will need to correct a whole lot less. Discipline is part of the character you build into your child that will give him a way of life.

Discipline and love go hand in hand. Many times parents tell a child just before a sound spanking, "This hurts me more than it does you," but the child absolutely does not believe it. Yet when discipline and love are bound together, it does hurt the parent. It causes him to understand in a small way how the heart of God must ache when He has to discipline His children repeatedly. Effective discipline is impossible without love. Love without discipline is spineless and not genuine; discipline without love is cold and militaristic. But when the two are joined together, the results are an effective tool for guiding, educating, and correcting children.

Guidelines for Discipline

Dr. Thomas P. Johnson, a psychiatrist for the San Diego County Probation Department, has written the following guidelines for parents. They are worth reprinting and he was kind enough to grant permission.

1. Don't disapprove of what a child is—disapprove of what he does.

2. Give attention and praise for good behavior—not bad behavior.

3. Encourage and allow discussion, but remember that it's the parents who should make the final decision.

4. Punishment should be swift, reasonable, related to the offense, and absolutely certain to occur—it need not be severe.

5. Throw out all rules you are unwilling to enforce and be willing to change the rules if and when you think they need changing.

6. Don't lecture and don't warn—youngsters will remember what they think is important to remember.

7. Don't feel you have to justify rules, although you should try to explain them.

8. As your youngster grows older, many rules may be subject to discussion and compromise. The few rules you really feel strongly about should be enforced no matter what rules other parents have.

9. Allow a child to assume responsibility for his decisions as he shows the ability to do so.

10. Don't expect children to demonstrate more self-control than you do.

11. Be honest with your youngster—hypocrisy shows.

12. The most important factor in your youngster's self-image is what he thinks you think of him. His self-image is a major factor in how he conducts himself.

Correction does not have a good effect on the child who hasn't been loved. The pain of punishment is not that effective. When the parent has developed a strong relationship with the child, then discipline that corrects will draw the parents and child closer together. His trust and admiration for his parent will reassure him in a time of correction that the parent is not doing it to seek revenge or to vent his anger. Rather, the child feels reassured that his parents truly care for him.

Many times our own children would be extremely loving immediately after a spanking. Rather than feeling fear at such a time, they experienced relief in the confidence that they had been restored to a good standing with their parents. When children have been well loved by their parents, the correction ignites a responding love in them that makes them want to become mature like their parents. Most of the time it makes them want to please their parents and be in good standing with them.

The first two years of a child's life are the most important years in which the parents' love arouses a response in children. It is in that period that his trust or mistrust and his respect or disrespect for authority are determined. Every Christian parent desires that his child grow up to be a responsible citizen and a God-fearing Christian. It takes training every hour, day, week, and month to build these important qualities in our children.

No mother can afford the high risk of letting someone else train her child during these crucial years. She needs to be with them for most of the day in their early childhood, to be ready to give comfort, love, and instruction when they need it most. They need the interaction between mother and child that occurs during the day for proper development during the preschool years.

For you single mothers who are required to work because you are the sole support of your child, I strongly urge you first of all to find a kind family member or friend who shares your values and to work out an arrangement with her.

If that is not possible, then the next best thing is to enroll your little one in a reputable Christian daycare center that will build Christian principles in his little heart. In addition, plan to spend as much of your nonworking and nonsleeping hours as you can doing things together that will build trust and respect in him.

Parents Have Temperaments Too

The way parents discipline their children is often a reflection of their own temperament. That is why some parents are prone to be strict disciplinarians and others are apt to be permissive. Most people marry partners that are opposite temperaments, and this presents conflicts when it comes to disciplining children. The passive partner will be accused of being too easygoing and the activist will be condemned because he is too strict. It is absolutely necessary for parents to come to an agreement on how they plan to discipline their children and then put into practice their united decision. There has to be a meeting of the minds to make discipline effective. Children will immediately recognize when their mom and dad do not agree, and they will begin to work one against the other.

Mary, for example, had been disobedient, and her father announced that she was on restriction for the whole weekend. I happened to be at their home when Mary told her mother she was going to a friend's house for the evening. The Choleric father said, "I thought you were on restriction, which means you are not allowed out of the house." The Sanguine mother quickly interfered by saying, "Oh, she is on restriction but she just has to leave a phone number where she is going."

I watched the father turn red in the face and his eyes flash. If I had not been present, I'm sure he would have exploded in rage. It was obvious that his wife was not reinforcing his discipline but rather was massaging it to suit herself. The daughter learned that day that her mom was an easy touch and that it was better to avoid going to her dad for permission. How much better it would have been if Mother had told Mary, "Your father and I have put you on restriction; therefore you must stay home tonight."

Four Responses

Let's take a look at a common problem that most homes are afflicted with and consider how the four different temperaments in parents would respond.

Fighting between brothers and sisters is as natural as water running downhill. (This seems to be a successful way that children have to worry parents.) It usually starts with one child being the aggravator, whether it be teasing or just "picking." It will not be long before words are going back and forth, then perhaps a shove or snatching away part of the game they were playing. Then the noise gets louder and sharper. Usually one child will end up in tears and go running to the parents screaming out accusations.

Who knows who is guilty and who has really started it? Chances are very good that neither child is innocent. But parents respond so differently to scenes such as this.

The Choleric parent is a strong disciplinarian and usually enforces any command that he gives. He will probably give one warning when he hears the battle begin to rage. After one warning to them to "stop this minute or I will give you both a sound spanking" and nothing has changed, he will storm into the room, grab them one at a time, and do just what he promised to do. He may even march them to the bedroom, lay them across the bed, and whack them both so they know that they have been spanked. This parent will give little explanation except "If I ever catch you fighting like that again, there will be more where that came from." The Choleric will be the most consistent on discipline but will be lacking in the love to go with it.

The Sanguine parent will warn the chldren 40 times to stop fighting. "Johnny, stop that!"—"Johnny, stop that!"—"If you don't stop that, I'll whip you!" but usually Johnny never gets whipped. Each time the warning will be louder and louder, until finally, between the children fighting and the parents screaming, you have a sound that resembles the "1812 Overture." At last this parent will rush into the room and either slap the children across the back or spank them on the spot, but unfortunately he has waited until he was overcome with anger before he did anything.

After the explosion has ended and the children are sobbing, the Sanguine parent will begin to feel very badly because of his explosion and his spanking in anger. Many times he will try to make up to the children by handing out candy or making some other gesture that will supposedly patch up everything. The Sanguine will be inconsistent in his discipline. One day the children will be spanked for their actions and the next day the same action will be overlooked.

The Melancholic parent will listen to the fighting and begin to feel as if he has failed. He will probably read into the scrap more than is there and will then go to the children on the verge of tears. "Why do you kids hate each other so?" or "Where have I failed?" or "Don't you kids realize what you're doing to me?" This parent will do a lot of talking and lecturing to these kids but will save the spanking for a last resort. Then he will feel guilty and remorseful and will indulge in self-pity that the children would do this to him. Probably the end result will be an "Excedrin No. 59 headache."

The Phlegmatic parent is the one who, whenever discipline is called for, tends to retreat from the scene of the action and hopes that his partner will solve the problem. He will either ignore the screaming or crawl into his shell as long as he can to tune out any trouble or violence.

When he finally decides that the children may kill each other if something isn't done, this parent will crawl out of his shell long enough to calmly say, "I'm going to give you one more chance," or "What will your father (or mother) say?" Spanking is so foreign to the Phlegmatic's nature that, if he is pressed into disciplining, he will probably set the children on a chair or send them each to their bedroom. More than likely a Phlegmatic mother will save the discipline until the father gets home. The Phlegmatic father will probably retreat to the garage until the storm passes.

Ephesians 6:4 NASB says, "Fathers, do not provoke your children to anger, but bring them up in the discipline and instruction of the Lord." This kind of training or discipline means guiding a child to help him mature and develop character with definite guidelines. It is more than giving him orders and lists of rules. Discipline should instruct, educate, guide, and train with faithful consistency. In the minds of many people, discipline merely means punishment as a means of getting a youngster to behave. There are two aspects of discipline—preventive and corrective. Corrective measures are absolutely necessary at times, but preventive measures will build self-discipline into your child.

Making Disciples

When you discipline your child, you are really training him to be a disciple. Dr. Henry Brandt says, "Parenthood is the process of making disciples of your children." In the early years he will be a disciple of you, his parents, and then as he matures and your teaching has laid the foundation, he will become a disciple of Jesus Christ. He will first be following your teaching and your example. How very important it is, then, that your teachings and your examples closely parallel those of Christ. Does your child see an undisciplined parent who is trying to tell him how to be disciplined?

The parent who does not assume the responsibility of disciplining his child is treating the child as though he were illegitimate, according to Hebrews. Hebrews 12:8 NASB says, "If you are without discipline, of which all have become partakers, then you are illegitimate children and not sons." An undisciplined child feels like he doesn't belong to anyone, and he suffers from not knowing how to obey.

22

Why Do Children Disobey?

There could be multiple reasons why a child disobeys, or it could be a single incident that is a temporary passing irritation. But for the child who repeatedly disobeys there has to be a weakness or a missing element in his development. We will consider the most common causes for disobedience and have listed below six basic reasons that a parent should examine. (You may think of more to add to this list.) Some children may have problems in all six areas while others lack in only one. Once you identify a missing element in your child's behavior, then you can plan and pray how you will begin to help him remedy the problem.

1. *He does not know the Lord personally.* This is the primary reason for disobedience and also the most important. It is very important that parents introduce their child to Jesus Christ at an early age. It won't solve everything, but a great deal of disobedience may be curbed when a child comes to Christ early in life because he will be at

ease with himself. The transforming work of Christ makes a great difference in the total being of even a young child.

2. *He has been allowed to feed the sins of the flesh.* The child who is permitted to selfishly demand his own way and to feed the lust of the flesh will become rebellious toward his parents. When he is allowed to read whatever he wants, watch any TV program he chooses, and see any movie (regardless of its rating), he will rebel against God.

It is outrageous to observe what is being shown on the movie screens across the world to decay the minds and lives of the viewers, and the highest percentage of the audiences are young people. I cannot understand mothers who carefully provide their children with clean linens, healthy foods, sterilized and polished silverware, etc., then turn around and allow them to feed their minds in the garbage pits of the world that will do more to contaminate and destroy their lives than sleeping on dirty linens or eating with dirty silverware.

Do you know what literature your child has been reading or what movies he has been seeing? One father decided for one month to watch every TV show his son watched and to see every movie at the theater his son went to see (that he was aware of). After 20 days the father decided he could not take any more. All of this was affecting his thought life and attitudes, and he felt he had stumbled on to why his son was becoming rebellious and argumentative. The wise parent will be aware of most of what the child feeds his mind and will carefully set guidelines.

3. *He has lived with a lack of parental discipline.* In other words, permissive parents have not fulfilled the role of

disciplinarians who love their children. The Bible says that the father is to be the head of the household and shall see that the children are brought up with discipline and instruction. All through the pages of Proverbs in the Old Testament are numerous verses that admonish parents to discipline and train their children in the ways of wisdom. The mother is to be the assistant and to fill in when the father is absent.

4. *He has not developed a spirit of submission.* Children best learn submission by watching—sons watching their fathers submit to God and daughters observing their mothers submit to their husbands. In order to be obedient, a child must have a submissive spirit. Disobedience must be corrected privately between the child and the parent, but restored publicly to the one he wronged.

For instance, in our children's early years we had such an episode. Two of our children were walking home from the grocery store with their father. On the way, he discovered that they each had a pocketful of little wrapped candies which he had not purchased. When he confronted them with the evidence, they both confessed to just helping themselves. The "rod of correction" was applied privately to each boy, and they all returned to the store to find the manager. The restoration came when they had to confess to him what they had done, ask his forgiveness, return the uneaten candy, and pay for the eaten ones out of their piggy banks. Correction like this teaches a submissive spirit and a response to authority.

5. *He is struggling for the affection and attention of his parents.* Unfortunately, a child discovers that one of the

quickest ways to get attention is to be disobedient. To the child who is starving for love and attention, the consequences of disobedience are worthwhile just to gain the attention of his parents, even if it is only temporary. Many active parents are so involved with their own goals in life that they fail to see these struggles in their children. The best-behaved children in school usually come from homes that are filled with family togetherness and lots of parental love.

6. *He has not been taught to respect authority.* Respecting authority begins with bridling the tongue, as we have stated previously in this book. Do you demand that your child speak to his parents and to other adults with respect? The child who has not been trained to respect the authority of his parents will have great difficulty in respecting the authority of his teachers, law officers, employers, and, most of all, his heavenly Father.

There is another unpopular subject that should be mentioned. Children may not respect authority because they do not see their mother being under submission to her husband, or they do not see their father showing love and respect to their mother. They will best learn by watching parental example. Where are the days when children were taught respect in answering their parents? Today their answers are usually "uh-huh" or "uh-uh," if you are lucky. It is not the actual words that are so important, but the respectful attitude and the discipline that accompany the answer. Before a child can give respect, he has to recognize who is in authority and who has the loving but controlling power.

Begin Now!

In closing this chapter, let me challenge you to begin now to respond to the six reasons a child disobeys. Examine the attitudes and responses of each of your children to see how each measures up to being an obedient child. If he scores high, then you are on the right path and are doing a good job in training up your child in the way he should go. Proper training does not require a great education, earthly possessions, or a high IQ. It simply requires diligence to your calling and obedience to God.

23

Practical Helps for Raising Children

The good and bad behavior of our children must be acknowledged for their proper development. When our children are good and well-mannered, we usually pay little attention to them. If they don't bother us, we don't bother them.

But when a child acts up, he gets your immediate attention. Instead of simply ignoring him when he is behaving well, try making a positive comment to him about something good he is doing. You might even be involved with his activity. Suggest to him how pleasant it is when everyone in the household is behaving and how he has made a real contribution to this good day.

Bad behavior can be changed in little children by reinforcing their good behavior. We can always find a reason to praise our children if we try hard enough. During a course of study in child development, I was assigned to do my laboratory work in a well-managed nursery school. One little boy in the school was a total terror to his teacher and the other youngsters in his class. We looked for something we could praise him for in an effort to motivate more cooperative behavior.

It took some time and consideration, but finally we found a solution. Each afternoon there was a rest period, and one day he happened to be doing what he was supposed to be doing—resting. (He was probably exhausted from harassing his family the night before.) The teacher captured this moment by announcing after the rest period that this little fellow was the best rester in the class that day. His mother later told us that he had informed the entire family that evening at dinner that he was the best rester in the whole class, because "the teacher said so."

For the next several days he rested quietly, something which he had never done before. Children respond to praise, and all children have some area in which they can be praised if we look hard enough.

How Effective Is Your Discipline?

It is wise to stand back and take a long look at the discipline you practice with your children and to carefully examine its quality and results. Know your child's temperament as you consider the kind of discipline needed for the offense. Unless a child understands what you expect of him, there is no way he can intelligently respond. The beginning of all discipline must begin with good, simple communication. The ultimate goal of parental discipline should be teaching the child self-discipline, and effective communication is the beginning step to reach that goal.

A good, basic plan for discipline will have these definite characteristics. Ask yourself the following questions:

1. *Is it constructive?* Discipline should result in helping the child rather than frustrating him. Proverbs 23:19 says, "Hear, my son, and be wise; and guide your heart in the way."

2. *Is it creating wise choices?* Discipline should guide and educate a child to make wise choices of his own. In doing this, you are helping him become self-disciplined. Proverbs 19:20 says, "Listen to counsel and receive instruction, that you may be wise in your latter days."

3. *Is it consistent?* True discipline means being faithful and consistent in responding to disobedience. Discipline that is carried out one time and overlooked the next time is not effective. Proverbs 29:17 says, "Correct your son, and he will give you rest; yes, he will give delight to your soul."

4. *Is it communicating love?* Discipline should spring from a heart of love for the child. It is also an assurance of being part of the family. Remember, "Whom the Lord loves He chastens" (Hebrews 12:6).

5. *Is it confidential?* The child needs to know that the discipline is between the parent and himself and that it won't become the topic of conversation at the next neighborhood coffee party. Jeremiah 31:34b says, "I will forgive their iniquity, and their sin I will remember no more." This confidence also builds into the child the belief that you have forgiven him and now all is forgotten.

There are several methods of creative disciplining, and the wise parent needs to select the appropriate one for each occasion.

1. *You may deprive the child of something very important to him.* This means depriving him of a privilege to do something that would be enjoyable for him. If Johnny takes the Play-Doh and consistently rubs it on the mahogany dining room table (and he is old enough to know better), then you might deprive him of the use of his Play-Doh for several days. Be sure you communicate to him that he has been told before (be sure that you have done this) not to put the clay on the furniture. The best way to help him remember this admonition is to take away the privilege of using it for several days. This will serve as a reminder that Play-Doh is not to be used on the good furniture but only at the special table designated by Mother.

2. *You may isolate the child from his friends or in his room.* It is important that you do not send him to his room as if he had to stay there forever. The purpose is to encourage him to make a change in his behavior, and when he feels he is able to do this he can go back and play. (Or else set the timer for a designated length of time.) After all, you could get busy and forget he is in confinement. Perhaps Sally has been an obnoxious tease with her friends to the point that she is causing constant turmoil. You should first communicate to her that she is causing trouble. Then inform her that she will have to go to her room and play by herself until she has decided that she can better control her actions. Always let her know that when she changes her behavior, she is welcome to go back and join her friends.

3. *You may let the child experience the natural consequences.* If you have communicated and it has not been effective, then you can turn to the unpleasant experience of allowing your child to reap the consequences. This cannot be allowed if it will cause severe harm to your child—you will have to weigh that potential. But remember, a little temporary physical pain is much better for our children than naggings and spankings that do not bring results.

For instance, Mary has a cruel habit of pulling the cat's tail. You have communicated to her time and time again, but to no avail. Then you finally decide that little Mary will have to experience for herself what happens when the cat's tail is pulled once too often. Even though she will undoubtedly suffer temporary pain, she will also learn through natural consequences that it is not wise to pull a cat's tail.

4. *You may use the "monetary reward system" for good and bad behavior.* This method has some very strong disadvantages. Probably the greatest is that it builds bad motivations. Some parents put charts on the wall that cover a week's worth of responsibilities. The children then accumulate points for completing what you expect them to do, such as making their beds, doing the dishes, taking out the trash, etc. When they neglect to do an assigned task, those points are subtracted from the week's total. The reward at the end of each week will be a certain amount of money for each point accumulated.

But most of us do not want our children to learn to do everything for money. They need to learn that there are certain things each member does just to carry his share of the load as a family member. The money method is a glorified form of bribery and does not allow the parent to get at the root cause of the child's lack of motivation or disobedience. How much better it would be to occasionally present him with a special bonus for willing cooperation when he spontaneously shares in the household responsibilities.

5. *You may have to spank the child.* Spanking should be reserved for willful defiance or when other methods have been ineffective. Spanking should not be used to teach a child responsibility. When spankings are administered for defiant disobedience and they are given as the Bible teaches, then a little signal is sent to the child's brain that says, "I had better not do that again."

There are right and wrong spankings. A wrong spanking would be a cruel, sadistic beating that is given in rage. This causes a child to be filled with anger and revenge and has not benefited him. A right spanking is given with a sound, positive approach. First, there needs to be communication on why the spanking will be given, and then it should be with a "rod" of correction and much love. One father had a paddle made with these words inscribed: "To my son with love." The Bible speaks clearly about the relationship of love and the "rod" of correction.

The Rod of Correction

Hebrews 12:11 says, "No chastening seems to be joyful for the present, but grievous; nevertheless, afterward it yields the peaceable fruit of righteousness to those who have been trained by it." The Bible gives sufficient instruction on how to discipline a child. It always refers to a rod when it speaks of correcting children. Below are listed some of the verses from Proverbs that speak about the rod of correction (or what you have selected to be your instrument of correction).

> He who spares the rod hates his son,
> But he who loves him disciplines him promptly.
>
> —Proverbs 13:24

> Foolishness is bound up in the heart of a child,
> But the rod of correction will drive it far from him.
>
> —Proverbs 22:15

> Do not withhold correction from a child,
> For if you beat him with a rod, he will not die.
> You shall beat him with a rod,
> And deliver his soul from hell.
>
> —Proverbs 23:13,14

> The rod and reproof give wisdom,
> But a child left to himself brings shame to his mother.
>
> —Proverbs 29:15

I firmly believe that God did not intend parents to use their hand for correcting except for slapping the hands of a very young child. Since he cannot understand your words, he will understand when his hand gets slapped as it reaches out for the electric plug.

The Bible continually refers to a "rod of correction." Children grow up to fear the rod, and when the rod you use for correction is your hand, then he fears the hand that will reach out to him in love and affection. Also, when a rod is used it gives you time to cool off if you are angry. After you have announced that it is necessary to use it, send a child to find it and you will have time to confess your anger and plan your next step before you start spanking him.

We would always send our children to get the "rod," which was a wooden spoon. It was surprising how that spoon was so difficult to find on many occasions, almost as though it had walked away! This form of punishment should only be used in extreme cases of disobedience or defiance.

Victory Over Anger

When I have discussed the subject of angry discipline with other parents, I have found that many times they spank spontaneously in anger with their hand, often striking the head, face, or hand of the child. Any discipline done in anger is very ineffective and wrong. This is responding with hurt, disappointment, or revenge, and none of these will instruct or educate a child to do right. The Bible warns against angry men (or women) and tells us to avoid them.

> Do not associate with a man given to anger,
> Or go with a hot-tempered man.
>
> —Proverbs 22:24 NASB

An angry man stirs up strife,
And a furious man abounds in transgression.

—Proverbs 29:22

A fool vents all his feelings,
But a wise man holds them back.

—Proverbs 29:11

He who is slow to wrath has great understanding,
But he who is impulsive exalts folly.

—Proverbs 14:29

He who is quick-tempered acts foolishly.

—Proverbs 14:17a

Parents who desire to practice effective discipline in their children will first have to get victory over their own anger and hot tempers. The Choleric and Sanguine parents will be more prone to outbursts of anger than the others. These parents need to confess that angry spirit to God and ask for help to change. "He who is slow to anger is better than the mighty, and he who rules his spirit than he who takes a city" (Proverbs 16:32).

A proper place has been designated in the Scripture where the rod of correction should be used. God has prepared a place on each child's anatomy with a fatty tissue that will cushion a severe spanking so as not to break bones or injure him. This area is at the base of the back and above the thighs, situated directly on the backside of every child. Proverbs refers to this spot and mentions its use.

> Wisdom is found on the lips of him who has under-
> standing,
> But a rod is for the back of him who is devoid of under-
> standing.
>
> —Proverbs 10:13

> Judgments are prepared for scoffers,
> And beatings for the backs of fools.
>
> —Proverbs 19:29

> A whip for the horse, a bridle for the donkey,
> and a rod for the fool's back.
>
> —Proverbs 26:3

How much better off children, families, and our nation would be if children were trained and disciplined according to the Proverbs guidebook.

24

The Value of Virtue

As we bring this discussion about our children to a close, I believe it is important to take a look at the world in which we are trying to raise our children.

The American family is faced with major challenges today, and what America has known as traditional family values has become a subject of national debate.

When the then-popular television celebrity Murphy Brown made a public showing of having a baby out of wedlock she fueled a national debate about unmarried mothers, and we clearly have a problem.

When sex education in the public schools is taught without any morals or values and condoms are handed out to our youth, we parents are faced with the very real threat that our children could be adversely affected, and we clearly have a problem.

When we cannot legally place a ban on the partial-birth abortion procedure, which is a violent crime against children, we clearly have a problem.

When the divorce rate is so high that well over 25 percent of our families are headed by single parents, most with no father in the home, we clearly have a problem.

When we have the growing demand from the homosexual community that they want to be allowed to legally marry and be recognized as a legitimate family, we clearly have a problem.

Starting at Home

The list could go on, but recognizing the deteriorating state of our society does not mean there is no hope for our children. It does mean, however, that the role that parents play in the lives of their children is more critical now than ever before. The place to start is inside our own homes.

We have given only a partial list of statistics about the immoral condition of our society, but there is something we can do about all this, and that is to start at home. There needs to be a concerted effort by all Christian parents and grandparents, including single parents, to teach our children the value of virtue.

What is virtue?

Virtue is moral excellence and righteousness.

A nation unravels without the value of virtue, and so does a family. When a nation denounces our godly heritage and the foundation of our country based on biblical principles, then it is inviting disaster. The same can be said of the family. A family invites disaster to their children when they fail to teach these values. Regardless of what blends of temperament your children might be, they all need to be taught moral excellence and righteousness.

Proverbs 14:34 says, "Righteousness exalts a nation, but sin is a reproach to any people." If sin disgraces a nation, then it could certainly be said about a family as well.

In examining your child's temperament and his needs, be sure to include the importance of teaching virtue. In other words, *teach him to excel in moral excellence and righteousness.* Such character traits as honesty, integrity, loyalty, sexual abstinence until marriage, and commitment to his future marriage partner are only a few of the very important values. But these will only be instilled as you dedicate yourself to be a living role model of moral excellence and to teach it to those who follow after you.

The Source of Greatness

A famous old adage applies to the virtue that we are addressing: "I sought for the greatness and genius of America in her commodious harbors and her ample rivers, and it was not there . . . in her fertile fields and boundless forests, and it was not there . . . in her rich mines and her vast world commerce, and it was not there . . . in her democratic Congress and her matchless Constitution, and it was not there. Not until I went into the churches of America and heard her pulpits aflame with righteousness did I understand the secret of her genius and power. America is great because she is good, and if America ever ceases to be good, she will cease to be great."

The same can be said of our families: It is only biblical righteousness that will keep our families great.